ON MODERN ART

Books by SALVADOR DALI

THE SECRET LIFE OF SALVADOR DALI

HIDDEN FACES

FIFTH SECRETS OF MAGIC CRAFTSMANSHIP

DALI ON MODERN ART

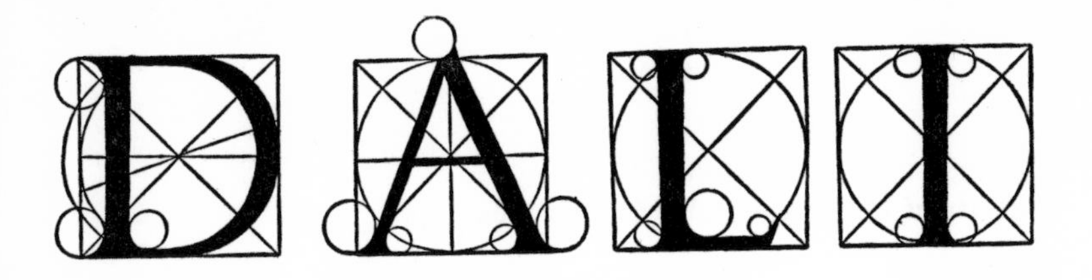

ON MODERN ART

The cuckolds of antiquated modern art

S. Dalí

Translated by HAAKON M. CHEVALIER

THE DIAL PRESS 1957 NEW YORK

Library of Congress Catalog Card Number: 57-14584

DESIGNED BY WILLIAM R. MEINHARDT
MANUFACTURED IN THE UNITED STATES OF AMERICA
BY THE HADDON CRAFTSMEN, SCRANTON, PENNA.

Avidadollars

André Breton

ON MODERN ART

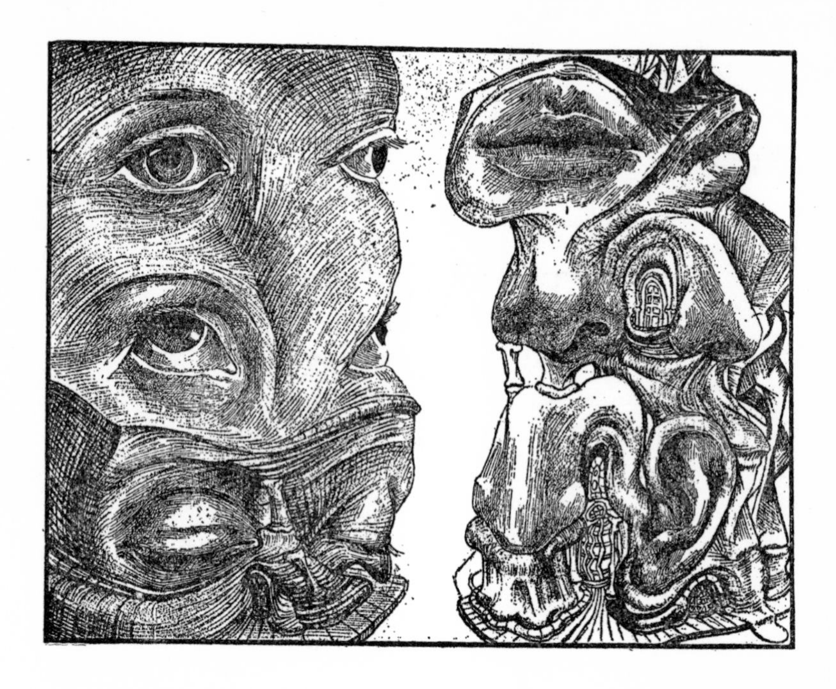

Architectonic project dated 1929, when I was defending the sublime genius of Gaudi in the face of the Protestant face of Le Corbusier.

Opening bars of Nietzsche's *Hymn to Friendship*

I EXPRESSLY WANT TO MAKE THIS communication in Paris, because France is the most intelligent country in the world, the most rational country in the world, whereas I, Salvador Dali, come from Spain, which is the most irrational country in the world, the most mystical country in the world.[1]

"Everyone knows that intelligence only leads us into the fog of scepticism, that its chief effect is to reduce us to factors having a gastronomical and supergelatinous, Proustian and gamey uncertainty. For which reasons it is well and necessary

[1] *In 1952, Dali wrote: "My country has an essential role to play in the great movement of 'nuclear mysticism' that is to mark our time. France will have a didactic role. She will probably draft the 'constitutive' act of nuclear mysticism by virtue of the prowess of her intelligence, but once again it will be Spain's mission to ennoble the whole by religious faith and beauty." (Editor's note).*

When I look at the starry sky, I find it small. Either I am growing, or else the universe is shrinking. Unless both are happening at the same time.

that Spaniards like Picasso and myself should come to Paris from time to time to dazzle you by putting a raw and bleeding piece of TRUTH before your eyes!"

It was with these words that I began my already excessively famous lecture at the Sorbonne on December 16, 1955, and it is exactly in the same manner that I intend to begin this lampoon, each new line of which is in the process of becoming classical, even if it be merely by the scratching of the paper on which I am writing.

The categorical heel-stamp of my pen, like a left leg, punctuates the haughtiest *zapateado,*[2] the *zapateado* of the jaws of my brain!

Olé!

[2] *The Spanish dancer marks the rhythm of his dance with sharp stamps of his heels and foot-beats in which Dali recognizes the hammerblows of his ideas.*

OLÉ! BECAUSE IT SO HAPPENS that the critics of the very antiquated modern art—who come from more or less central Europe, in other words from nowhere —are letting their most succulently Rabelaisian ambiguities and their most truculently Cornelian errors of situation in speculative cookery simmer in the Cartesian cassoulet.

The least magnificent ideological cuckolds[3]—with the exception of the Stalinian cuckolds—are two in number:

First: the old dadaist cuckold whose hair is turning white, who receives a diploma of honor or a gold medal for having tried to assassinate painting.

[3] *In Littré's Dictionary we find the following example given: "It was said that a married man whose wife was unchaste was called* cocu *(a cuckold), after a fine bird who is called a* cocu, *and by others a* couquon, *so named from its song; and for the reason that this fine bird goes and lays its eggs in the nests of other birds, being so stupid that it is incapable of making one for itself, so by antithesis and contrariety is he called a cuckold in whose nest another comes and lays an egg, that is to say begets offspring." Boucher. (Editor's note).*

From THE FATES. *Pediment of the Parthenon.*

Since the well-nigh divine beginnings of the reclining body its decline follows an inclined slope.

From GIORGIONE. *Venus.*

In the Renaissance it is still quite beautiful, though the Dionysiac and Gaudinian side of vital tragedy is absent.

From INGRES. *The Odalisk.*

With Ingres it is still intact, but the French Revolution has passed, and bourgeois taste has appeared. Ingres resists.

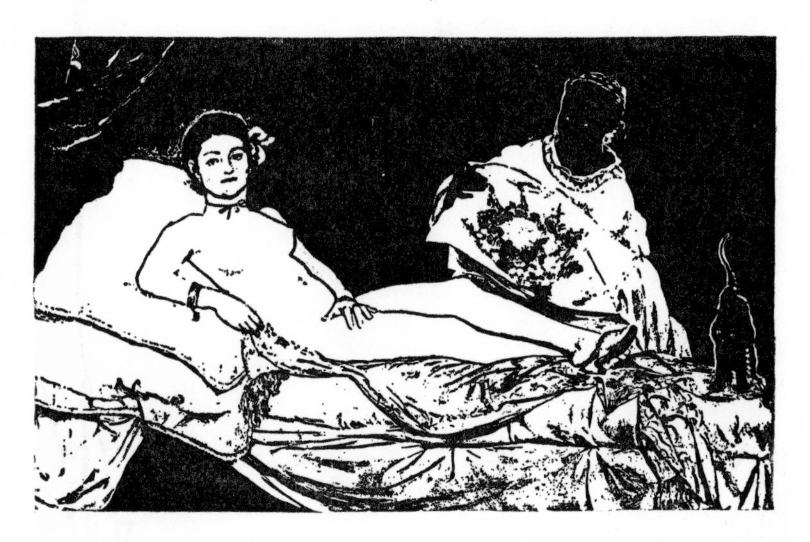

From MANET. *Olympia.*

Things are in a bad way . . .

With Matisse we shall witness the apotheosis of bourgeois taste.

*Ingres: the last painter who knew how to paint—was the integrity of his drawing.**

* *A reference to Ingres' oft-quoted dictum: "Drawing is the integrity of art"* (Le dessin est la probité de l'art). *(Translator's note).*

From ROUSSEAU. *The Dream* (Yadwigha).

After naturalism, only the naïve was lacking; to do full justice to it this artist isolates the detail of the nude.

From PICASSO. *Reclining Nude.*

Grave in the extreme, cannot possibly get worse, pure bestiality.

Were it not for the extravagant titles that he gives to his canvases, Mr. Dali's painting would no longer be worth bothering with.

The critic of the *New York Times*

Second: the almost congenital cuckold, the dithyrambic critic of antiquated modern art, who straight away auto-recuckolds himself by dadaist cuckolding.

Since the dithyrambic critic has contracted marriage with antiquated modern art, the latter has been constantly unfaithful to him. I can mention at least four examples of this cuckolding:

1) He has been betrayed by the ugly.
2) He has been betrayed by the modern.
3) He has been betrayed by the technical.
4) He has been betrayed by the abstract.

The introduction of the ugly into modern art began with the romantic adolescent naïveté of Arthur Rimbaud, when he said, "Beauty seated herself on my knees and I grew weary of her." It is by virtue of these keywords that the dithyrambic critics—negativistic to the *n*-th degree, and hating classicism like any self-respecting sewer rat—discovered the biological agitations of the ugly and its unavowable attractions. They began to marvel at a new beauty, which they claimed to be "unconventional," and beside which classical beauty suddenly became synonymous with quaintness.

All ambiguities became possible, including that of savage objects, ugly as mortal sins (which is what they really are). In order to remain attuned to the dithyrambic critics, painters dedicated themselves to the ugly. The more of it they turned out, the more modern they were. Picasso, who is afraid of everything, went in for the ugly because he was afraid of Bouguereau.[4] But he, unlike the others, went in for it on purpose, thus cuckolding those dithyrambic critics who claimed

[4] *Bouguereau, Adolphe-William, to quote the Twentieth-Century Larousse. Born in 1825, died in 1905. Covered with diplomas and gold medals, he is regarded as the general of conventionalists. But he is a discredited general who*

The actualizing of African, Lapp, Lett, Breton, Gallic, Majorcan or Cretan arts is but an effect of modern cretinization. It's all Chinese, and God knows how little I like Chinese art.

to be rediscovering true beauty. Only as Picasso is an anarchist, after having knifed Bouguereau half to death, he was going to give the *puntilla,*[5] and finish off modern art at one blow by out-uglying, alone, in a single day, the ugly that all the others combined could turn out in several years.

For the great Pablo, the angelic Raphaël, the divine Marquis de Sade and I—the rhinocerontesque Salvador Dali—actually have the same idea as to what an archangelically beautiful being may represent. This idea, in fact, in no way differs from the one instinctively possessed by any crowd in the street—bearer of the heritage of Graeco-Roman civilization—when it turns round, petrified with admiration at the passage of a body—let us call a spade a spade—of a Pythagorean body.

At the algid[6] moment of his greatest frenzy of ugliness, I sent Picasso the following telegram from New York:

> Pablo thanks! Your last ignominious paintings have killed modern art. But for you, with the taste and moderation that are the very virtues of French prudence, we should have had painting that was more and more ugly, for at least one hundred years, before reaching your sublime adefesios esperentos.[7] You, with all the violence of your Iberian anarchism, have achieved the limits and the

---

still inspires fear. One day Picasso asked a friend of his how he liked his latest work, a collage *made of pieces of newspaper. When his friend remained speechless the master, beside himself, found the telling formulation. "It may not be sublime," he said, "but at least it's nothing like Bouguereau." (Editor's note).*

[5] *Next to the dance, bullfighting is Dali's favorite source of images. He is certainly a Spaniard. (Editor's note).*

[6] *The* algid *period of cholera is the period during which the patient suffers from chill. (Editor's note).*

[7] *The phrase is Picasso's own. Literally it means "persons who are ugly and ridiculous as scarecrows." But it is probable that Picasso combines this idea with a certain phantasmagoric immateriality. (Editor's note).*

From PICASSO. *The Woman with the Fish-hat.*
It's not that beautiful.

From BOUGUEREAU. *Birth of Venus.*
It's not that frightful.

Picasso wanted to be a communist. He has nevertheless remained the king of us all. In ten years it will be said that as a painter Picasso was not that good, and Bouguereau not that bad. One day Picasso said to me, "In any case, we are as good and as useful as those buffoons whom the kings of Spain used to keep in their courts and whose opinions they respected." To which I replied, "We are today the only beings possessed of a royal will."

final consequences of the abominable in a mere few weeks. And this you have done, as Nietzsche would have wished, by marking it with the seal of your own blood. Now all that remains for us is to turn our eyes once more to Raphael. God preserve you!

Salvador Dali.

All this ended up in the false Cartesian and scatological explosion of Dubuffet. But the dithyrambic critics of antiquated modern art remained and will long continue to remain prostatic and joyous with the ugly seated on their knees. They will not grow weary of it.

Buffet, more quaint than Puvis de Chavannes, is scarcely even ugly.

From B. BUFFET. *Two Female Nudes.*
It won't get any worse, for Picasso has killed all this.

From PUVIS DE CHAVANNES. *The Poor Fisherman.*
Buffet would paint this two hundred years hence if he had the talent of Puvis de Chavannes.

Dali has had the courage, at the height of the "modern" period, to strive to emulate Meissonnier and he has nevertheless succeeded in painting like Dali!

THE CRITICS OF ANTIQUATED MODern art have especially been led astray and cuckolded by the "modern" itself. Nothing, in fact, has ever aged more rapidly and more poorly than all that they at one moment qualified as "modern."

When I was barely twenty-one years old, I happened to be having lunch one day at my friend Roussy de Sales' in the company of the masochistic and Protestant architect Le Corbusier who, as everyone knows, is the inventor of the architecture of self-punishment. Le Corbusier asked me if I had any ideas on the future of his art. Yes, I had. I have ideas on everything, as a matter of fact. I answered him that architecture would become "soft and hairy" and I categorically affirmed that the last great genius of architecture was called Gaudi whose name, in Catalan, means "enjoy," just as Dali means "desire." I explained to him that enjoyment and desire are characteristic of Catholicism and

With his paranoiac-critical method Dali has contributed to surrealism a first-rate weapon.

André Breton

of the Mediterranean Gothic, reinvented and brought to their paroxysm by Gaudi. In listening to me, Le Corbusier had the expression of one swallowing gall.

Later, the very "modern" *Cahiers d'Art* were to launch an attack on Gaudi, of a perfectly modern mediocrity. To defend him I wrote some masterly pages, worthy of an anthology, on *Modern Style* and the Paris subway entrances. I cannot resist the desire to reproduce these in their entirety, as they appeared in number 3-4 of the *Minotaure*.*

Colossal, ravishing incomprehension of the phenomenon

The readily literary utilization of the "1900" style tends to become frightfully continuous. To justify it a pleasant, much-quoted formula is used, mildly nostalgic, mildly comical, capable of provoking a "kind of smile" that is peculiarly repulsive: I mean a discreet and witty "Laugh, Clown, laugh," based on the most lamentable mechanisms of "sentimental perspective" by virtue of which it is possible, with a very exaggerated distance, to judge by contrast a relatively close period. In this manner anachronism, in other words the "delirious concrete" (sole vital constant) is presented to us (in consideration of the intellectualist aestheticism attributed to us) as the essence of the "ephemeral out of its accustomed surroundings" (ridiculous—melancholy). It can be seen that what is involved is an "attitude" based on the smallest, the least arrogant "superiority complex," accompanied by a coefficient of "sordid-critical" humor that makes everyone happy and enables

* *This article was called "As of the Terrifying and Edible Beauty of Modern Style Architecture."* (Editor's Note.)

Painter, if you want to ensure for yourself a prominent place in Society you must, in the first flush of your youth, give it a violent kick in the right leg.

anyone who wants to display concern with preserved artistic-retrospective realities to appraise the unheard-of phenomenon with the prescribed and decent facial contractions. These facial contractions, treacherous reflexes of "repression-defense," will have the effect of inducing an alternation of benevolent and understanding smiles—tinged, to be sure, with the indispensable well-known tear (corresponding to "conventional memories," simulated ones)—and bursts of laughter, frank, explosive, irresistible though devoid of vulgarity, every time one of those violent, hallucinating "anachronisms" appears, whether in connection with one of those tragic and grandiose edible sado-masochistic costumes or, even more paradoxically, with one of those terrifying and sublime Modern Style ornamental architectures.

I believe I was the first, in 1929 and at the beginning of *La Femme visible,* to consider the delirious Modern Style architecture as the most original and the most extraordinary phenomenon in the history of art, and I did so without a shadow of humor.

I here emphasize the essentially extra-plastic character of Modern Style. To my mind, any use of the latter for properly "plastic" or pictorial ends could not fail to imply the most flagrant betrayal of the irrationalist and essentially "literary" aspirations of these movements. The "replacement" (a question of fatigue) of the "right-angle" and "golden section" formula by the convulsive-undulating formula can in the long run only give rise to an aestheticism as melancholy as the preceding one—momentarily less boring because of the change, and that is all. The best subscribe to this formula: a curved line appears today to become once more the shortest distance between two points,

Since my first childhood I have had a vicious turn of mind that makes me consider myself different from the common run of mortals. This still persists, and I have never failed to thrive by it.

and the most vertiginous—but all this is but "the ultimate wretchedness of plasticism," an antidecorative decorativism, contrary to the psychic decorativism of Modern Style.

Apparition of the Cannibal Imperialism of Modern Style

The "manifest" causes that have produced Modern Style still appear to us too confused, too contradictory and too vast to make it possible to determine them at the present time. The same could be said for its "latent" causes, although the intelligent reader may be led to deduce from what will be said that the movement that concerns us was mainly aimed at awakening a kind of great "original hunger."

Like the determination of its "phenomenological" causes, any attempt at an historical elucidation concerning it would encounter the greatest difficulties, especially by reason of that contradictory and rare collective sentiment of ferocious individualism that characterizes its genesis. Let us therefore limit ourselves today to noting the "fact" of the brusque apparition, of the violent irruption of Modern Style, testifying to an unprecedented revolution in the "sense of originality." Modern Style, in fact, appears as a leap, with all the most cruel traumatisms for art that such a leap may entail.

It is in architecture that we shall have an opportunity of marveling at the deep shattering, in its most consubstantially functionalist essence, of every "element" of the past, even the most congenital, the most hereditary. With Modern Style the architectural elements of the past, aside from the fact that they will be subjected to the frequent, to the total convulsive-formal

Painter, do not concern yourself with being modern. It is the only thing, unfortunately, no matter what you do, that you cannot avoid being.

grinding that will give birth to a new stylization, will be called upon to live again, to subsist currently in the true aspect of their origins, so that in combining with one another, in melting into one another (despite their most intellectually irreconcilable and irreducible antagonisms) they will reach the highest degree of aesthetic depreciation, will manifest in their relations that frightful impurity that has no other equivalent or equal than the immaculate purity of oniric intertwinings.

In a Modern Style building, Gothic becomes metamorphosed into Hellenic, into Far-Eastern and, should it occur to one—by a certain involuntary whim—into Renaissance which in turn may become pure, dynamic-asymmetrical (!) Modern Style, all in the "feeble" time and space of a single window, that is to say in that time and that space, little-known and probably vertiginous, which as we have just insinuated, are none other than those of dreams. Everything that was the most naturally utilitarian and functional in the known architectures of the past suddenly ceases, in Modern Style, to serve any purpose whatever or, which is hardly calculated to win over pragmatist intellectualism, serves only for the "functioning of desires," these being, moreover, of the most turbid, disqualified and unavowable kind. Grandiose columns and medium columns, inclined, incapable of holding themselves up, like the tired necks of heavy hydrocephalic heads, emerge for the first time in the world of hard undulations of water sculptured with a photographic scrupulousness of instantaneity until then unknown. They rise in waves from the polychrome reliefs, whose immaterial ornamentation congeals the convulsive transitions of the feeble materializations of the most fugitive metamorphoses of smoke, as well as aquatic

I sing your longing for limit eternal!

Federico Garcia Lorca

vegetations and the hair of those new women, even more "appetizing" than the slight thirst caused by the imaginative temperature of the life of the floral ecstasies into which they vanish. These columns of feverish flesh (37.5°C.) are destined to support nothing more than the famous dragon-fly with an abdomen soft and heavy as the block of massive lead out of which it has been carved in a subtle and ethereal fashion, a block of lead such (by its ridiculous excess of weight which nevertheless introduces the necessary idea of gravity) as to accentuate, aggravate and complicate in a perverse way the sublime sentiment of infinite and glacial sterility, to render more comprehensible and more lamentable the irrational dynamism of the column, which as a result of all these circumstances of delicate ambivalence cannot fail to appear to us as the true "masochistic column" having solely the function of "letting itself be devoured by desire," like the actual first soft column built and cut out of that real desired meat toward which Napoleon, as we know, is always moving at the head of all real and true imperialisms which, as we are in the habit of repeating, are nothing but the immense "cannibalisms of history" often represented by the concrete, grilled and tasty lamb-chop that the wonderful philosophy of dialectical materialism, like a new William Tell, has placed on the very head of politics.

Thus in my view it is precisely (I cannot emphasize this point too strongly) the wholly ideal Modern Style architecture that incarnates the most tangible and delirious aspiration of hyper-materialism. An illustration of this apparent paradox will be found in a current comparison, made disparagingly it is true, yet so lucid, which consists in assimilating a Modern Style house

to a cake, to a pastry-cook's exhibitionistic and ornamental tart. I repeat that this is a lucid and intelligent comparison, not only because it emphasizes the violent materialist-prosaicism of the immediate, urgent needs on which ideal desires are based, but also because by this very fact and in reality, the nutritive and edible character of this kind of house is thus alluded to without any euphemism, these houses being nothing other than the first edible houses, the first and only erotizable buildings, whose existence verifies that urgent "function," so necessary to the amorous imagination: to be able quite really to eat the object of desire.

Modern Style, Phenomenal Architecture
General Characteristics of the Phenomenon

Deep depreciation of intellectual systems.—Highly accentuated depression of the reasoning activity, to a degree bordering on mental debility.—Positive lyrical imbecility.—Total aesthetic unconsciousness.—No lyrical-religious coaction; on the other hand: release, freedom, development of the unconscious mechanisms.—Ornamental automatism.—Stereotype.—Neologisms.—Great childhood neurosis, refuge in an ideal world, hatred of reality, etc.—Delusion of grandeur, perverse megalomania, "objective megalomania."—Need and feeling for the fanciful and hyperaesthetic originality.—Absolute shamelessness of pride, frenzied exhibitionism of "caprice" and imperialist "fantasy."—No notion of restraint.—Realization of solidified desires.—Majestic blossoming with erotic, irrational, unconscious tendencies.

Psychopathological Parallel

Invention of "hysterical sculpture."—Continuous erotic ecstasy.—Contractions and attitudes without antecedents in the history of statuary (reference is to the women discovered and known after Charcot and the school of la Salpêtrière).—Confusion and ornamental exacerbation in relation to pathological communications; dementia praecox.—Close affinities with the dream-world; reveries, waking fantasies.—Presence of characteristic oniric elements: condensation; displacement, etc.—Development of the anal sadistic complex.—Flagrant ornamental coprophagia.—Very slow, exhausting onanism, accompanied by an enormous sense of guilt.

Extra-Plastic Concrete Aspirations

The sculpture of everything that is extra-sculptural: water, smoke, iridescences of pre-tuberculosis and nocturnal pollution, woman-flower-skin-peyotl-jewels—cloud-flame-butterfly-mirror. Guadi built a house patterned on the forms of the sea, "representing waves on a stormy day." Another is built of the still waters of a lake. I am not indulging in idle metaphors, fairy-tales, etc., these houses actually exist (Paseo de Gracia in Barcelona). I am speaking of real buildings, a real sculpturing of reflections of twilight clouds in water, made possible by recourse to an immense and insane multicolored and gleaming mosaic of pointillist iridescences from which emerge forms of spread water, forms of water puckered by the wind, all these forms of water built in an asymmetrical and dynamic-instantaneous succession of reliefs, broken, syncopated, en-

twined, fused by the "naturalist-stylized" water lilies and nympheals being materialized in impure and annihilating eccentric convergences by thick protuberances of fear, spurting from the incredible façade, contorted both by all the demential suffering and by all the latent and infinitely sweet calm that is equaled only by that of the horrifying apotheosic and ripe furuncle ready to be eaten with a spoon—with the bleeding, fat, soft spoon of gamey meat that is approaching.

The point was thus to build a habitable structure (one which, moreover, as I claim, should be edible) with the reflections of twilight clouds on the waters of a lake, the work having in addition to embody a maximum of naturalistic exactness and optical illusion. I proclaim that this is a gigantic improvement on the mere Rimbaldian submersion of the drawing-room at the bottom of a lake.

Return to Beauty

Erotic desire is the ruin of intellectualist aesthetics. Where the Venus of logic vanishes, the Venus of "bad taste," the "Venus in furs" appears beneath the banner of the only beauty, that of real vital and materialist agitations.—Beauty is but the epitome of consciousness of our perversions.—Breton has said, "Beauty shall be convulsive or nothing." The new surrealist age of the "cannibalism of objects" likewise justifies this conclusion: "Beauty shall be edible or nothing."

Salvador DALI

TODAY, TWENTY YEARS AFTER THIS article in *le Minotaure,* I have won the battle for Gaudi, for my friends Alfred Barr,[1] director of the Museum of Modern Art in New York, and Sweeney, of the Museum of Non-Objective Art, have recognized his genius by writing one of the most important books about him. And the admiration that Le Corbusier himself feels for Gaudi[2] he has transcended in his own architecture, which is wholly to his honor.

But it is easier to approximate the genius of Gaudi than

[1] *Alfred Barr was one of Dali's earliest friends. It was he who persuaded him to come to the United States. In his* Secret Life *Dali says of him: "His jerky gestures reminded one of those of pecking birds. And what he was in fact doing was to peck and scratch about among contemporary values, judiciously selecting the sound grain and separating it from the chaff." (Editor's note).*

[2] *In 1935, during the Barcelona uprising, Gaudi's body was exhumed and dragged through the streets by urchins. The friend who described the scene to Dali added that Gaudi looked very well embalmed and preserved, but seemed at the moment to be a bit under the weather. (Editor's note).*

The least that one can ask of a piece of sculpture is that it should not move.

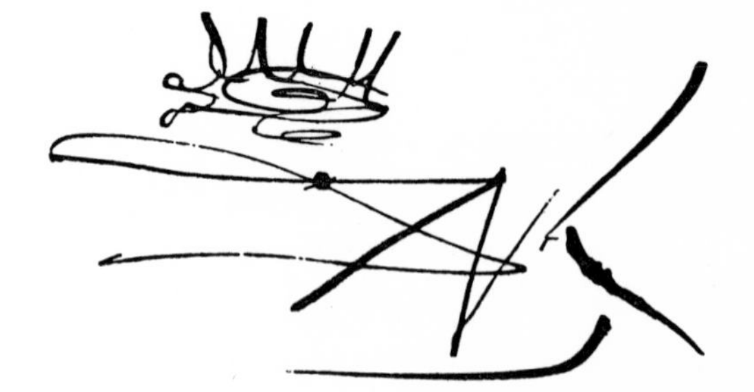

that of Raphael, the first being a genius surrounded by the thunder of cataclysms and the other a genius bathed in celestial silence. What is now to be won is the battle for Raphael, the most decisive and the hardest of all. It is only in the just appraisal of Raphael that the true superior spirits of our epoch can be recognized, since Raphael is the most anti-academic, the most tenderly living and the most futuristic of all the aesthetic archetypes of all times.

I ask of my friends Le Corbusier, Barr and Sweeney, and especially Malraux, that they pause a moment to examine how terribly one of those glued, yellow, anecdotic, literary and sentimental papers of the cubist period has aged, both physically and morally! Let them compare it to the little Saint George by Raphael,[3] which has remained fresh as a rose! But I am not sanguine of the result, for these four are still too much on the side of the cataclysm!

But, whether solicited by cataclysm or heaven, our moderns could not endure the least vestiges of ornamentation in their "dwelling machines" and they have been invaded by abstract academicism which is only very mediocre pseudo-decorative art.

Our moderns, whose hair bristles with horror at the idea of a matter that is not aseptic and prefabricated, have not had to wait till the end of their lives to witness the apotheosis of the most naïve folklore, the resurrection of all plagiarisms, of all archeologisms of all times, on the sole condition that these be soiled and falling apart. Every self-respecting modern painting, piece of pottery or carpet must seem to have come from an excavation and simulate the accidents of patina and truculent decrepitude. And this to a point that one would not have tol-

[3] *In the Mellon collection in Washington. (Editor's note).*

Something comes to an end with the death of that painter of seaweed just barely suitable for helping the bourgeois digestion—I mean Matisse, the painter of the revolution of 1789.

erated in the time of the lamented "Michelangelo buffets," when one contented oneself with imitating modest worm-holes.

And after all, what is more cuckolded, more betrayed, more afflicted with cracks than this modern art with its mania for the sterilized cleanliness of functional forms and aseptic surfaces, whereas one would think it was plague-ridden and had been found, by an irony of destiny, as they say, in those garbage cans where the Italian Burri goes rummaging for blood-stained rags. Even though eternally and blithely cuckolded, Burri none the less suspends above his head those pieces of refuse that have the form of the most depressing of all "mobiles" like those that a "first prize-winner" in modern—modern—sculpture makes to order for him.

Advocates of the ultra-new, snubbed by the parvenus of the pseudo old-old, the dithyrambic critics have been led astray by technique; with Impressionism the decadence of pictorial art became . . . impressive.

Paul Cézanne—one of the most marvelously reactionary painters of all time—was also one of the most "imperialistic," since he wanted to redo Poussin "from nature," hence according to the new conception of the discontinuity of matter, the great truth of the Dionysiac divisionism of Impressionism. It is unfortunate that his Apollonian impulse[4] was betrayed by his fatal clumsiness. His awkwardness can be compared only to the delirious virtuosity of Velasquez. It should have been Velasquez who, like Bonaparte, poured the anarchy of orgiac painting into the

[4] *It will be recalled that in Nietzsche's philosophy "Apollonian" designates one who has the faculty of creating real images. Whereas in the same philosophy, "Dionysiac" is used of the state in which man is conscious of himself as capable of representation or intelligence. (Editor's note).*

Even as Voltaire with the Heavenly Father, Braque and I bow to each other, but we do not speak!

Caesarian empire of forms, adding that notion of discontinuous nature that Poussin lacked.

But, however touching it may be, never did Cézanne succeed in painting a single round apple capable of holding—monarchically—the five regular bodies[5] within its absolute volume.

The dithyrambic critics, completely in line with the mediocrity of Cezannian paintings, were only able to set up as categorical imperatives the catastrophic deficiencies, clumsinesses and awkwardnesses of the master. Before this total rout of means of expression it was believed that a step had been taken toward the liberation of pictorial technique. Every failure was baptized economy, intensity, plasticity—and when that horrible word, "plasticity," is uttered, it means that the worms are already at work!

In short, deceived but gay as usual, the dithyrambic critics, instead of finding themselves in possession of the noble basket of intact and divine apples—the symbol of a new Cezannian golden age—were simply left alone with a basket filled with their own shit.[6] And since, even to weave a simple basket with dignity a certain technique remains indispensable, they had succeeded in fabricating only a kind of basket utterly unworthy of the name. Never can Michel de Montaigne's expression, "to shit[7] in one's basket and then put it on one's head," be more

[5] *That is to say: the cube, the tetrahedron, the dodecahedron, the hexahedron and the octahedron. (Editor's note).*

[6] *"In ancient Rome no difficulty was made over speaking of shit. Horace, the delicate Horace, and all the poets of the century of Augustus, speak of it in a hundred places in their works." (Comte de Caylus).*

[7] *Another example of the use of this rare word: "Here lies a king, wonderful to relate, who died, as God wills, by the blow of a brush-hook and an old woman as he was shitting into a chest." (d'Aubigné).*

The two geniuses of creative forms (dynamism of the discontinuity of matter instantaneously congealed) are the Italian Boccioni and the Catalan Gaudi, who have made of Milan and Barcelona the capitals of the industrial revolution.

wisely applied than to those dithyrambic critics of the new technique of modern painters.

Barely had they been successively betrayed by the "ugly" and the "modern," then by "technique," than our dithyrambic critics were once more, without being given any respite, cuckolded then and there by "abstract art." But this time the cuckolding was colossal, totalitarian, imperial, I would almost say cosmic both in its spiritual aspect (so thoroughly blasted that nothing worse could happen to it) and in its temporal aspect, for it is no longer a mystery that those who had put their faith in it are in the process of losing all their money, a sure sign of bankruptcy.

The deceit began with Picasso whose Andalusian blood bore in its current pieces of that monument of iconoclasm which is the Alhambra of Granada. Then cubism went about smashing matter into smithereens, still using the materials of the "neo-Platonic mason" that Cézanne made use of to keep his houses standing up. To this cubism was to add a little cement from Huerta del Ebro in Aragon, for the earth of Aragon is the most ferociously realistic and concrete in the world.

It is not difficult, on looking back, to see that the materials used by Cézanne, plus those materials furnished to cubism by the earth of Aragon, were Catholic *par excellence,* and that it was only with them that it was going to be possible to paint reality. A certain Arab coquetry would, moreover, reveal itself perfectly adequate to fragment the too dry and too peeled Hispano-Moorish form, just as the impressionists had decomposed light with the moist subtlety that falls from the skies of Delft. How, too, could one fail to recognize this subtlety in

From VERMEER. *The Music Lesson.*

It is more beautiful than what has been said about it and more beautiful than anything we believe about it.

From MONDRIAN. *Composition.*
Piet "Niet."

Juan Gris, you are the categorical executioner of the Discourse on the Cubic Form *by Juan de Herrera, the architect of Philip II of Spain. The Escurial, like yourself, is realism and mysticism made architecture. Juan Gris, I like you very much! With Seurat, you are the most classic of the moderns.*

the maternal and Atlantic reminiscences and regrets of Velasquez, whose mother was Portuguese, which explains the miracle of the painting of the greatest of all artists: the virile member of Castille forever wet with an ejaculation that only the granitic veins of Spain could conduct by mysterious channels to the painter's pupil.

Cubism thus was and remains merely the most heroic effort to preserve the object (genius and object to the grave) at the moment when a full consciousness of the new discontinuity of matter was being acquired. In point of fact, the concern continued to be with objects, ever with objects, concrete and anecdotic objects that came to bear the labels of their own sentimental anecdote. The guitars are of cement, their angles cut hands and faces with the objective grinding of their structures. All this objectivity carried to its paroxysm is not glaringly obvious to the aestheticians who regard it as a stage in the direction of the abstract rather than a revolt of the object.

There is nothing abnormal in this, and Picasso once confessed to me privately that none of the panegyrists of his gray cubism had ever been able to see what his paintings represented. Hence from these monstrous academicisms were born all the neo-plasticisms and in particular that degrading example of mental debility that was pompously called "abstraction-creation."

And so one was to hear the Piet, Piet, Piet of the new modern academicians. This Piet Mondrian, however, had a soft spot for Dali. He used to say that no one in the world was capable as I was of placing a small stone that projects its shadow in the space of a painting. I in turn have a soft spot for Mondrian, for as I adore Vermeer I find in Mondrian's order the

Piet Piet Piet Piet Piet
Piet Piet Piet Piet Piet
Piet Piet piet piet
piet Piet Piet Piet Piet piet Piet
Piet piet piet piet piet piet Piet
piet piet Piet Piet

chamber-maid's cleanliness of Vermeer and even his retinian instantaneity of blues and yellows. I nevertheless hasten to say that Vermeer is almost everything and Mondrian almost nothing!

Completely idiotic critics have for several years used the name of Piet Mondrian as though he represented the *summum* of all spiritual activity. They quote him in every connection. Piet for architecture, Piet for poetry, Piet for mysticism, Piet for philosophy, Piet's whites, Piet's yellows, Piet, Piet, Piet.......
..........................Piet, Piet, Piet, Peep, Pity, Piet. Well, I Salvador, will tell you this, that Piet with one "i" less would have been nothing but a *pet,* which is the French word for fart.[8]

[8] *"Suddenly Epistemon began to breathe, then to open his eyes, then to yawn, then sneeze, then let a large household fart." (Rabelais, II, 30).*

Of all the pupils of Gustave Moreau, the best will always be the one who taught them.

AN ARAGONESE *jota* HAS THIS strident refrain, a visceral, Iberian and irrational cry:

> "I love you as one loves one's mother
> as one loves money!"

What I like best in all the philosophical writings of Auguste Comte is the precise moment where, before founding his new positivist religion, he places the bankers, whom he regards as of capital importance, at the summit of his hierarchy. Perhaps this is the Phoenician side of my Ampurdan blood, but I have always been dazzled by gold in whatever form it appears. Having learned in my adolescence that Miguel de Cervantes, after having written his immortal *Don Quixote* for the greater glory of Spain, died in wretched poverty, that Christopher Columbus, after having discovered the New World, had also

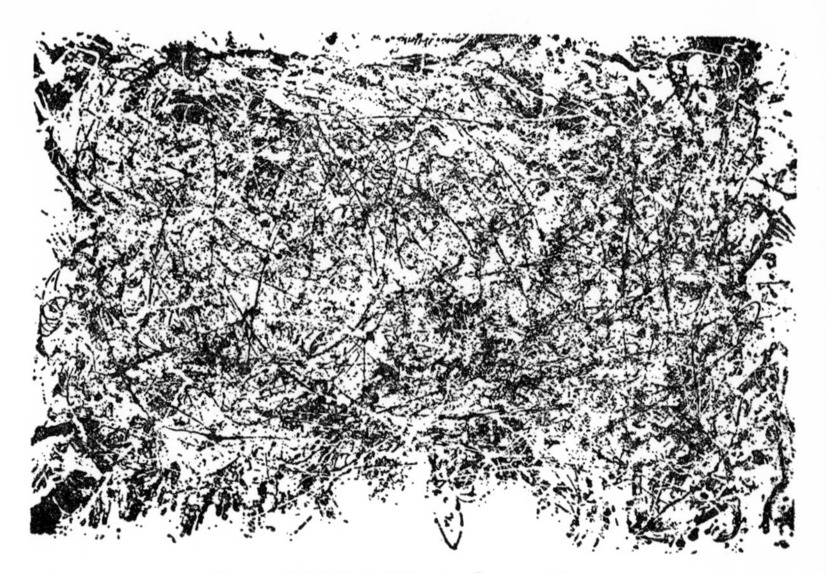

From POLLOCK. *Jackson, No. 1.*
The same fish-soup as Monticelli, but far less tasty, merely the indigestion that goes with it.

From MONTICELLI. *The Fountain.*
Fish-soup for fish-soup's sake.

died under the same conditions, and in prison to boot, already in my adolescence, as I say, my prudence strongly counseled me two things:

1) to have my prison experience as early as possible. And this was done.

2) to become to the greatest extent possible a bit of a multimillionaire. And this, too, is done.

The simplest way of refusing any concession to gold is to have some oneself. With gold it becomes quite unnecessary to "engage oneself." A hero does not engage himself anywhere! He is the very opposite of a servant. One really must have teeth covered with Sartre not to dare to speak like this! So let us be prudent, as Saint-Granier[1] recommends, if we want to permit ourselves to be Nietzschean. All the concrete values of modern painting will remain eternally translatable on the material level into that thing that I personally have always loved: *money!*[2]

In compensation, the pure critics who have consistently despised money and been afraid to dirty their hands by touching it may rest assured: the abstract values that they defend in modern paintings will inevitably be converted into absolutely clean,

[1] *A Paris radio commentator who broadcasts a daily one-minute program in which he deals in a folksy, common-sense way with everyday problems. (Translator's note).*

[2] *As everybody knows, André Breton baptized Dali "Avida Dollars." Dali claims that this anagram was his talisman which made "the rain of dollars fluid, gentle and monotonous." He has promised himself some day to tell the whole truth about this blessed profligacy of Danaë. It will form a chapter of a new book to be entitled "The Life of Salvador Dali Considered as a Masterpiece." (Editor's note).*

Without the slightest hesitation, without a doubt, the worst painter in the world is called Turner.

wholly inoffensive and immaterial money. It will be purely abstract money.

END

S. S. AMERICA

EN ROUTE TO LE HAVRE. APRIL 1956.

EPILOGUE

Children have never particularly interested me, but the thing that has interested me even less is the drawings of children.

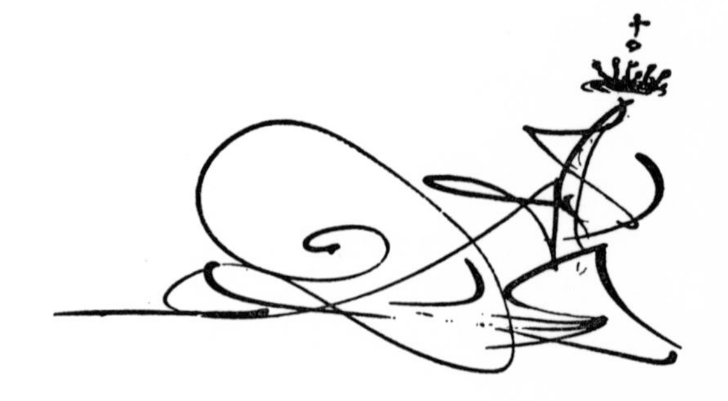

IN THE WHOLE MODERN REVOLUTION one single idea has not aged and remains so living that it will be the foundation of the new classicism that is imminently awaited. None of the dithyrambic critics of antiquated modern art has yet noticed it. It involves nothing less than Paul Cézanne's famous *from nature.*[1]

The Discontinuity of Matter

The most transcendent discovery of our epoch is that of nuclear physics regarding the constitution of matter. Matter is discontinuous and any valid venture in modern painting can and must proceed only from a single idea, as concrete as it is significant: *the discontinuity of matter.*

This discontinuity is announced for the first time in the history of art by Vermeer's corpuscular touches and Velasquez's

[1] *Nature is the name that the painter gives to physics. (Editor's note).*

*Miro, who basely tried to murder painting, had the courage to let himself be eaten by folklore.**

* *He is nevertheless the best in his field, for the good reason that he is a Catalan!* (S.D.)

brush-strokes in the air. Likewise, it is impressionism which for the first time invented the division of light. Seurat's chromosomatic confetti are the notarized act of the discontinuity of matter. The sadistic collision of complementaries in the perimeter—broken up by the Brownian movement—of Cézanne's apples, is but the physical manifestation of the movement of discontinuous matter.

In Picasso's gray cubism, the reintegrative parceling of reality is but an example of the ferocious determination of this reality to preserve a figurative aspect in the very discontinuity of matter. The visceral wrenches of the gifted Boccioni are the foreshadowing of the supersonic dynamism and the glorious Apollos of the discontinuity of matter. Duchamp's "King and Queen" we may pass through rapidly because of the discontinuity of matter. Dali's watches are soft because they are the masochistic product of the discontinuity of matter. Mathieu's signs are the royal decrees of the discontinuity of matter.

The dionysiac swarming is there, but all this heroic heterogeneity will remain aesthetically worthless so long as the artistic and classical form of an Apollonian cosmogony has not been found.

If the vitally heterogeneous and anti-academic forces of modern art are not to perish in the anecdotic absurdity of sheer experimental and narcissistic dilettantism, three essential things are needed:

1. Talent, and preferably genius.[2]

[2] *Since the French Revolution a vicious cretinizing tendency has developed which consists in considering that geniuses (aside from their work) are in every respect beings more or less like other common mortals. This belief is false. I affirm this for myself who am the outstanding modern genius. (S.D.)*

Dali, what a fanatic!

SIGMUND FREUD

2. Learning again how to paint as well as Velasquez and preferably as Vermeer.[3]

3. The possession of a monarchic and Catholic cosmogony, as absolute as possible and having imperialist tendencies.

Only then, like Nietzscheans in reverse, that is to say aspiring to the sublime, shall we observe with the naked eye, "from nature," the antiprotonic archangel so divinely burst that we shall at last be able to plunge our painter's hands between the *fissioned* chromosomes of his nightingalesque substance and with our aching and blood-swollen fingers touch the discontinuous treasure desired since our own youth. And, believing with Soeringe that we control everything by our potential will to power, I know that we shall then touch our own divinity as painters.[4]

Read, approved and signed:
Salvador DALI.

[3] *In his* Mystical Manifesto *that appeared in 1952, Dali was already telling painters: "Painters, paint meticulously with as much reality as a color photograph, let your hand behave like a stroboscope, and then I promise you that from that moment your paintings will have a chance of becoming immortal!" (Editor's note).*

[4] *It may perhaps have been noticed that Dali the writer is not sparing in his admiration for Dali the painter, but this is because he is convinced of the "monarchic" superiority of the painter in general. Three years ago the Iberic anarchist Federation published a manifesto to announce its support of the Spanish monarchy—for, it was specified, painters are monarchs. Herein Dali recognizes one of his most cherished ideas: there is real freedom only under the authority of a monarch. In his childhood he was very fond of wearing a regal disguise, but it is not to this title that he aspires for himself, it is to the one conferred upon him by his given name, Salvador, the savior of painting. In his* Diary of a Genius, *as yet unpublished, he observes, among other things: "Before going to sleep, instead of rubbing my hands (this abominable gesture would be typically anti-Dalinian) I kiss them with a very pure joy, telling myself all the while that the universe is a slight thing compared to the amplitude of a brow painted by Raphael." (Editor's note).*

"I consider Picasso a very great painter. I have fifteen of his canvases in my collection, but never will he paint a picture to equal Dali's Cena, *for the very simple reason that he is not capable of doing so."*

CHESTER DALE, President of the
National Gallery in Washington.

APPENDICES

APPENDIX

DALI'S LUCIDITY WHEN HE SPEAKS of painting is enough to discourage critics who never approach the question otherwise than from the outside. In reply to a survey on the emancipation of painting, Dali, as early as 1934, stated:

"If I am to express myself briefly on the questions of the 'model,' of the 'spontaneity' and of the element of 'chance' in the painted work, I shall say that in my opinion—and to attempt to make these few words as substantial as possible—the 'model' should be for the painter only a succulent and gelatinous 'gratinéd pig's foot' in which, as everyone knows, the soft and superfine meat merely envelops the true and authentic peeled bone of objectivity with its 'deliria of nutritive sweetness.' But the best gratinéd and the most savory of all pig's feet which, if one makes the slightest appeal to memory, is that of 'realism,' happens to have been scented centuries ago by the fine

Painters, do not fear perfection. You will never achieve it! If you are mediocre, and you do your utmost to paint very, very badly, it will still be evident that you are mediocre.

noses of the Dutch painters and finally eaten by Vermeer of Delft, who left only the cold bone, so that the great Meissonnier in licking it could discover its last delicate succulence. If in our day there is no longer any 'model' there is every reason to believe that it is because the painter ate it, and this is too generally and too popularly admitted to make it necessary for me to insist on the inevitable nostalgia of every painter before every model. How could the pig's foot in question still exist today, when we know that the surrealists, going beyond the cannibalism of meat, have passed on to that of bones, finally reaching the point of devouring objects and object-beings? From all of which you can gather that the model can exist for me only as an intestinal metaphor. Not only the model, but even objectivity itself has been eaten. I can therefore paint only according to certain systems of digestive delirium.

"As concerns spontaneity, I shall say that it too is a pig's foot, but a pig's foot in reverse, that is to say a crayfish which, as everyone knows, unlike the pig's foot, presents an external skeleton, while the superfine and delicate meat, that is to say the delirium, occupies the interior, which means—to speak in a single spurt and without euphemism—that, for spontaneity, the carapace of objectivity offers a resistance to the soft delirium of the meat; that, in order to reach the latter, one often loses time and that in addition one reaches it only to discover that the meat which one finds has no bone. All these considerations lead me to be generally suspicious of 'spontaneity' in its pure state, in which I always recognize the conventional and stereotyped taste of the invariable restaurant crayfish, and personally to prefer, rather than spontaneity, "systematization" which, like paranoiac delirium, can occur and in fact does occur 'spontaneously'—the

'spontaneity' in question having ceased to lay claim to an *undiscoverable objectivity,* especially as it has been previously destroyed, as we have seen in the case of the crayfish, but on the contrary implying that supplementary succulence, the most delicate of all, which resides in the taste and even in the contact of the meat that can still be found and that is found within the bones, when after the bone has been gnawed, the moment of attacking it appears. It is precisely at the algid moment when one reaches the very marrow of the imagination that one has the right to assume that one dominates (as in fact one does dominate) the situation.

"If the 'model' is a gratinéd pig's foot and spontaneity a crayfish, chance could well be merely a serious and important grilled lamb-chop, bubbling with savor and biological ulterior motives. I say this advisedly, because chance represents and constitutes exactly that middle point of succulence between the 'model' and 'spontaneity,' that is to say between the gratinéd pig's foot and the crayfish *à Iarmoricaine.* It will in fact be observed that if in the pig's foot the bones are inside the meat and in the crayfish the meat within the skeleton, in the case of the lamb-chop the bones are half inside, half outside, that is to say coexistent, and that the bone and the meat, objectivity and delirium, showing visibly at the same time, do nothing but set forth this truth that I shall never weary of repeating, namely that chance is nothing other than the result of a systematic irrational (paranoiac) activity; which, to come back to our edible obsessions and to our vocabulary borrowed from nutrition, can be summarized in the idea that chance, as it manifests itself in the artistic phenomenon, is merely the expression of the conflict, terribly exciting for famine, which results from our

ELUARD: *So much confusion to remain pure!*

RENÉ CREVEL: *With Bonapartist Trotskyism, he will* renecrevel.*

* *Untranslatable pun on René Crevel's name:* crever *means to croak— He will croak, but in his own personal style. (Translator's note).*

being exposed simultaneously to the bone and the meat, to specify once again: to objectivity and to delirium, further aggravated by that ardor of the grilled meat burning one's teeth (every grilled lamb-chop worthy of the name having to be eaten so hot that it burns one's teeth, but this is another matter) and when I say 'burning one's teeth' I mean 'burning one's imagination.' "

BRETON: *So much intelligence for such a tiny downfall!*

ARAGON: *So much climbing to reach such a negligible height!*

APPENDIX II

Around the Birth of a Film

IN 1954 AT THE LOUVRE MUSEUM, Salvador Dali executed a copy of *The Lacemaker* by Vermeer of Delft, a painting whose aggressive power had obsessed him since his childhood. On the canvas Dali painted rhinoceros horns which he was to continue the following spring, but this time at the Zoo in Vincennes before a living rhinoceros. Having returned to Spain, he finished this rhinocerontic and corpuscular copy during the summer of 1955 and in December of the same year delivered a lecture at the Sorbonne in Paris, to explain the affinities, morphological on the one hand and on the other

cosmogonic,[1] discovered by him between the *Lacemaker,* the rhinoceros, the sunflower and the cauliflower.

At the time of the visit to the Louvre Museum, Robert Descharnes undertook the making of a motion-picture film, "The Prodigious Story of the *Lacemaker* and the Rhinoceros," and since then has been making a film record of all Salvador Dali's delirious and systematic investigations and actions.

In this cinematographic "adventure," while Salvador Dali's evolution as a painter is described by means of a certain number of shots of his most important canvases from the surrealist period to the present, the picture does not deal so much with his painting as such, but rather with Dali's evolution, from surrealism to his present paintings (and thereby to his attitude toward contemporary painting).

Thanks to Dali's collaboration, to his genius for correspondences and to the extraordinary systematization of his delirium, "The Prodigious Story of the *Lacemaker* and the Rhinoceros" will be the first film dealing with critical-paranoiac activity;[2] Robert Descharnes attempts to show its development in Dali's life and to explain the application of this method both to his painting and to parallel investigations, like those that lead from Vermeer's *Lacemaker* to gooseflesh[3] via the rhinoceros and the cauliflower.

In order to have the shots that are to show this genius for

[1] *By cosmogonic should be understood "pertaining to the cosmogony (or mythology) peculiar to Dali." (Editor's note).*

[2] *Spontaneous method of irrational knowledge based on the critical interpretative association of delirious phenomena. (Editor's note).*

[3] *For Dali it is primarily the corpuscular divisionist aspect that is the link between Vermeer and this* microphysical *gooseflesh. (Editor's note).*

correspondences and double images[4] keep their full visual effectiveness, the usual camera tricks and devices have been systematically ruled out.

[4] *"It is by a frankly paranoiac process that it is possible to obtain a double image, that is to say the presentation of an object which, without the slightest figurative or anatomical modification, is at the same time the representation of another, absolutely different object, likewise free of any kind of deformation or abnormality that might conceal some arrangement." (René Crevel:* Dali or Anti-obsurantism*).*

Dalí

LES COCUS DU VIEIL ART MODERNE

LES COCUS
DU VIEIL ART
MODERNE

Début de l'hymne à l'amitié, de NIETZSCHE.

JE TIENS EXPRESSÉMENT À FAIRE cette communication à Paris, parce que la France est le pays le plus intelligent du monde, le pays le plus rationnel du monde, tandis que, moi Salvador Dali, je viens de cette Espagne qui est le pays le plus irrationnel du monde, le pays le plus mystique du monde.[1]

Chacun sait que l'intelligence ne nous fait déboucher que dans les brouillards du scepticisme, qu'elle a pour effet principal de nous réduire à des coefficients d'une incertitude gastronomique et supergélatineuse, proustienne et faisandée. C'est

[1] *En 1952, Dali écrivait déjà: «Le rôle de mon pays est essentiel dans le grand mouvement de «mystique nucléaire,» qui doit marquer notre temps. La France aura un rôle didactique. Elle rédigera probablement l'acte «constitutif» du mysticisme nucléaire grâce aux prouesses de son intelligence, mais encore une fois ce sera la mission de l'Espagne d'ennoblir tout par la foi religieuse et la beauté.»* (N. d. E.)

pour ces raisons qu'il est bon et nécessaire que, de temps à autre, des Espagnols comme Picasso et moi, nous venions à Paris pour vous éblouir en vous mettant sous les yeux un morceau cru et saignant de VÉRITÉ! . . .»

C'est par ces mots que je commençai ma déjà très célébrissime conférence à la Sorbonne le 16 décembre 1955, et c'est exactement de la même manière que j'entends commencer ce libelle dont chaque nouvelle ligne est en train de devenir classique, ne serait-ce que par les crissements du papier sur lequel j'écris.

Le coup de talon catégorique de ma plume scande comme une jambe gauche le *zapateado*[2] le plus hautain, le *zapateado* des mâchoires de mon cerveau!

Olé!

[2] *Le danseur espagnol rythme sa danse de secs coups de talon et de piétinements dans lesquels Dali reconnaît les martèlements de sa pensée.*

OLÉ! PARCE QUE LES CRITIQUES du très vieil art moderne—venus des Europes plus ou moins centrales, donc de nulle part—font précisément mijoter dans le cassoulet cartésien leurs équivoques les plus savoureusement rabelaisiennes et leurs erreurs de situation les plus truculemment cornéliennes de cuisine spéculative.

Les cocus[1] idéologiques les moins magnifiques—exception faite des cocus staliniens—sont au nombre de deux:

Primo: le vieux cocu dadaïste à la chevelure blanchissante, qui reçoit un diplôme d'honneur ou une médaille d'or pour avoir voulu assassiner la peinture.

[1] *Dans Littré, on trouve cité cet exemple: «Il fut dit qu'on appelait un homme marié cocu, qui avait une femme impudique, d'un bel oiseau qu'on appelle cocu, les autres l'appellent couquon, ainsi nommé de son chant; et pour ce que ce bel oiseau va pondre au nid des autres oiseaux, estant si sot qu'il n'en saurait faire un pour luy, par antithèse et contrariété on appelle celui-là cocu, au nid duquel on vient pondre, c'est-à-dire faire des petits.»* Bouchet. (N. d. E.)

Secundo: le cocu quasi congénital, critique dithyrambique du vieil art moderne, qui s'auto-recocufie d'emblée par le cocufiage dadaïste.

Depuis que le critique dithyrambique s'est marié avec la vieille peinture moderne, cette dernière n'a cessé de le tromper. Je puis citer au moins quatre exemples de ce cocufiage:

1) Il a été trompé par la laideur.
2) Il a été trompé par le moderne.
3) Il a été trompé par la technique.
4) Il a été trompé par l'abstrait.

L'introduction de la laideur dans l'art moderne a commencé avec l'adolescente naïveté romantique d'Arthur Rimbaud, quand il a dit: «La beauté s'est assise sur mes genoux et je m'en suis fatigué.» C'est grâce à ces mots-clés que les critiques dithyrambiques—négativistes à outrance, et haïssant le classicisme comme tout rat d'égout qui se respecte—découvrirent les agitations biologiques de la laideur et ses inavouables attirances. Ils commencèrent à s'émerveiller d'une nouvelle beauté, qu'ils disaient «non conventionnelle,» et à côté de laquelle la beauté classique devenait soudain synonyme de mièvrerie.

Toutes les équivoques étaient possibles, y compris celle des objets sauvages, laids comme les péchés mortels (qu'ils sont en réalité). Pour rester à l'unisson des critiques dithyrambiques, les peintres travaillaient à faire du laid. Plus ils en faisaient, plus ils étaient modernes. Picasso qui a peur de tout, fabriquait du laid par peur de Bouguereau.[2] Mais lui, à la différence

[2] *Bouguereau, Adolphe-William, dit le Larousse du XXe siècle. Né en 1825, mort en 1905. Couvert de diplômes et de médailles d'or, il passe pour le général*

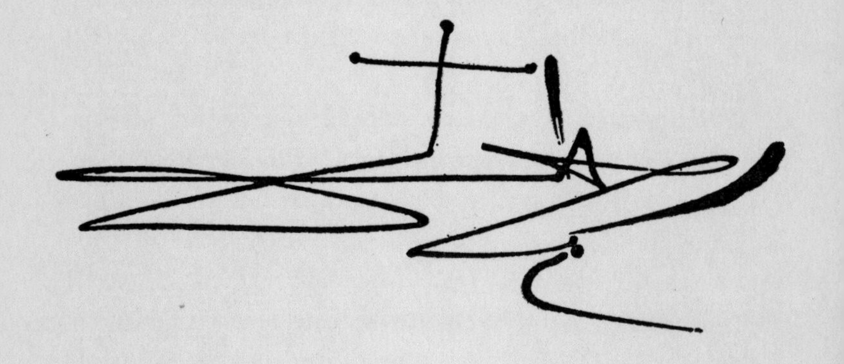

des autres, en fabriquait exprès, cocufiant ainsi ces critiques dithyrambiques qui prétendaient retrouver la vraie beauté. Seulement comme Picasso est un anarchiste, après avoir à moitié poignardé Bouguereau, il allait donner la *puntilla,*[3] et achever d'un coup l'art moderne en faisant plus laid à lui seul en un jour qu'en plusieurs années tous les autres réunis.

Car le grand Pablo avec l'angélique Raphaël, le divin marquis de Sade et moi—le rhinocérontesque Salvador Dali—se fait la même idée de ce que peut représenter un être archangéliquement beau. Cette idée ne diffère d'ailleurs en rien de celle que possède d'instinct n'importe quelle foule de la rue—héritière de la civilisation gréco-romaine—quand elle se retourne pétrifiée d'admiration, sur le passage d'un corps—appelons les choses par leur nom—d'un corps pythagoricien.

Au moment algide[4] de sa plus grande frénésie de laideur, j'envoyai, de New York, à Picasso le télégramme suivant:

> «Pablo merci! Tes dernières peintures ignominieuses ont tué l'art moderne. Sans toi, avec le goût et la mesure qui sont les vertus mêmes de la prudence française, nous aurions eu de la peinture de plus en plus laide, pendant au moins cent ans, jusqu'à ce qu'on arrive à tes sublimes

---

des pompiers. Mais, c'est un général décrié qui fait encore peur. Un jour où Picasso faisait admirer à un de ses amis sa dernière œuvre, un collage de morceaux de journaux, comme cet ami restait sans voix, le maître, n'y pouvant plus tenir, trouva le mot décisif: «Ce n'est peut-être pas sublime, mais, en tout cas, ce n'est pas du Bouguereau.» (N. d. E.)

[3] *Après la danse, c'est à la tauromachie que Dali a recours pour ses images. C'est bien un Espagnol.* (N. d. E.)

[4] *Période* algide *du choléra, période du choléra dans laquelle le malade est glacé.* (N. d. E.)

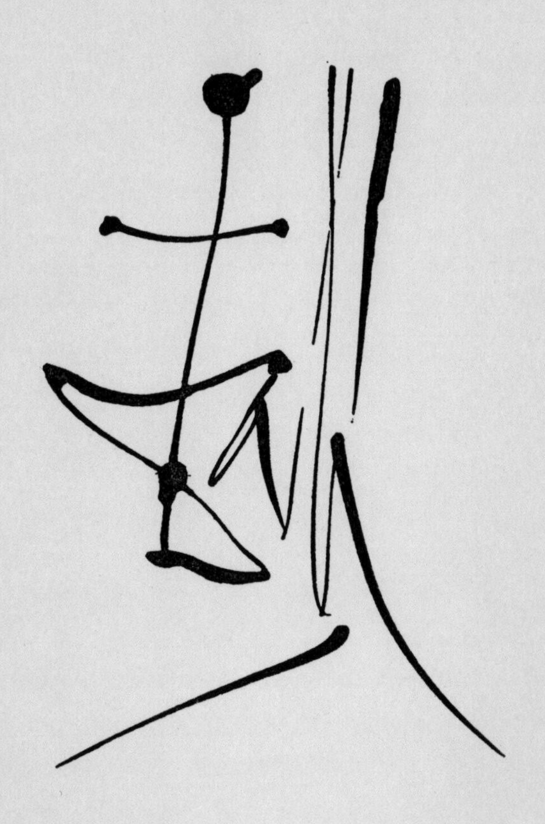

adefesios esperpentos.[5] Toi, avec toute la violence de ton anarchisme ibérique, en quelques semaines tu as atteint les limites et les dernières conséquences de l'abominable. Et cela, comme Nietzsche l'aurait voulu, en marquant tout de ton propre sang. Maintenant, il ne nous reste plus qu'à tourner de nouveau nos yeux vers Raphaël. Que Dieu te garde!»

Salvador Dali.

Tout cela trouva pour fin la fausse explosion cartésienne et scatologique de Dubuffet. Mais les critiques dithyrambiques du vieil art moderne restent et resteront encore longtemps prostatiques et joyeux avec la laideur assise sur leurs genoux. Ils ne s'en fatigueront pas.

[5] *Le mot est de Picasso lui-même. Littéralement, il signifie: «personnages laids et ridicules comme des épouvantails.» Mais il est probable qu'à cette idée Picasso joint celle d'une certaine immatérialité fantasmagorique.* (N. d. E.)

Les critiques du vieil art moderne ont été surtout égarés et cocufiés par le «moderne» même. Effectivement rien n'a jamais vieilli plus vite et plus mal que tout ce qu'à un moment ils qualifièrent de «moderne.»

Alors que j'avais à peine vingt et un ans, je me suis trouvé un jour à déjeuner chez mon ami Roussy de Sales en compagnie de l'architecte masochiste et protestant Le Corbusier qui est, comme on le sait, l'inventeur de l'architecture d'auto-punition. Le Corbusier me demanda si j'avais des idées sur l'avenir de son art. Oui, j'en avais. J'ai d'ailleurs des idées sur tout. Je lui répondis que l'architecture serait «molle et poilue» et j'affirmai catégoriquement que le dernier grand génie de l'architecture s'appelait Gaudi dont le nom, en catalan, signifie «jouir,» de même que Dali veut dire «désir.» Je lui expliquai que la jouis-

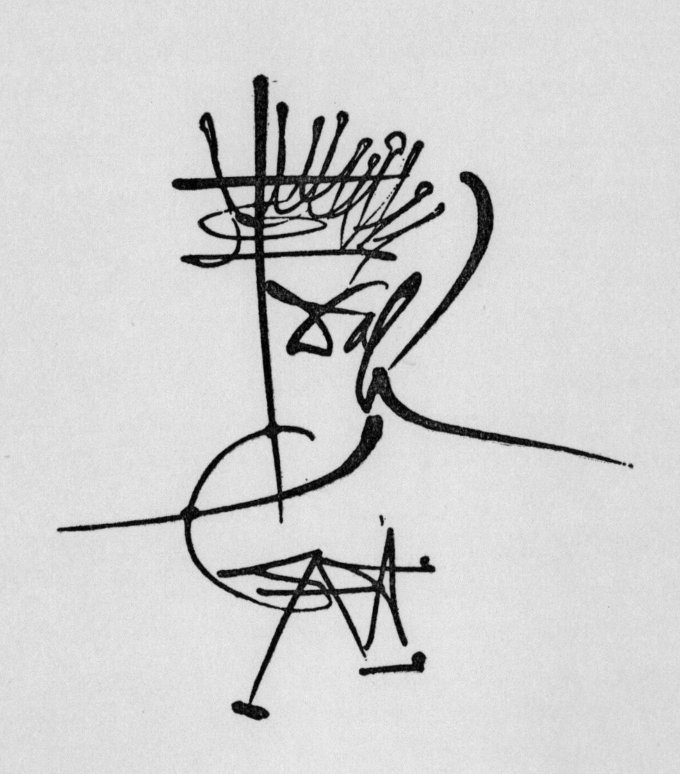

sance et le désir sont le propre du catholicisme et du gothique méditerranéens réinventés et portés à leur paroxysme par Gaudi. En m'écoutant, Le Corbusier avait l'air d'avaler du fiel.

Plus tard, les très «modernes» *Cahiers d'Art,* devaient déclencher une attaque d'une médiocrité parfaitement moderne contre Gaudi. Pour le défendre, j'écrivis des pages magistrales, dignes d'une anthologie, sur le *Modern'Style* et les bouches de métro. Je ne résiste pas à l'envie de les reproduire intégralement telles qu'elles parurent dans le numéro 3-4 du *Minotaure.**

Incompréhension colossale, ravissante du phénomène

L'utilisation facilement littéraire du «1900» tend à devenir affreusement continue. On se sert pour la justifier d'une formule aimable, à succès légèrement nostalgique, légèrement comique, susceptible de provoquer une «espèce de sourire» particulièrement répugnant: il s'agit d'un discret et spirituel «Ris donc, Paillasse,» fondé sur les mécanismes les plus lamentables de la «perspective sentimentale» grâce auxquels il est possible de juger par contraste, avec un recul très exagéré, d'une époque relativement proche. De cette manière l'anachronisme, c'est-à-dire le «concret délirant» (unique constante vitale) nous est présenté (en considération de l'esthétisme intellectualiste qu'on nous prête) comme l'essence de «l'éphémère dépaysé» (ridicule —mélancolique). Il s'agit, comme on voit, d'une «attitude» fondée sur le plus petit, sur le moins orgueilleux «complexe de supériorité» auquel vient s'ajouter un coefficient d'humour «sordide-critique» qui rend tout le monde content et permet à quiconque veut montrer le souci des confites actualités

* *De La Beauté Terrifiante et Conestible de l'Architecture Modern'Style."*

artistiques-rétrospectives d'apprécier le phénomène inouï avec les contractions faciales réglementaires et décentes. Ces contractions faciales, réflexes, traîtresses, de «refoulement-défense» auront pour effet de faire alterner les sourires bénévoles et compréhensifs—teints, il est vrai, de l'indispensable larme bien connue (correspondant aux «souvenirs conventionnels,» simulés)—et les rires francs, explosifs, irrésistibles quoique non révélateurs de vulgarité, chaque fois qu'apparaît un de ces «anachronismes» violents, hallucinants, qu'il s'agisse d'un de ces tragiques et grandioses costumes sado-masochistes comestibles ou, plus paradoxalement encore, d'une de ces terrifiantes et sublimes architectures ornementales du Modern'Style.

Je crois avoir été le premier en 1929 et au début de *La Femme visible,* à considérer, sans l'ombre d'humour, l'architecture délirante du Modern'Style comme le phénomène le plus original et le plus extraordinaire de l'histoire de l'art.

J'insiste ici sur le caractère essentiellement extra-plastique du Modern'Style. Toute utilisation de celui-ci à des fins proprement «plastiques» ou picturales ne manquerait pas d'impliquer pour moi la trahison la plus flagrante des aspirations irrationalistes et essentiellement «littéraires» de ces mouvements. Le «remplacement» (question de fatigue) de la formule «angle-droit» et «section d'or» par la formule convulsive-ondulante ne peut à la longue que donner naissance à un esthétisme aussi triste que le précédent—moins ennuyeux momentanément à cause du changement, c'est tout. Les meilleurs se réclament de cette formule: la ligne courbe paraît redevenir aujourd'hui le plus court chemin d'un point à un autre, le plus vertigineux—mais tout cela n'est que la «misère dernière du plasticisme.»

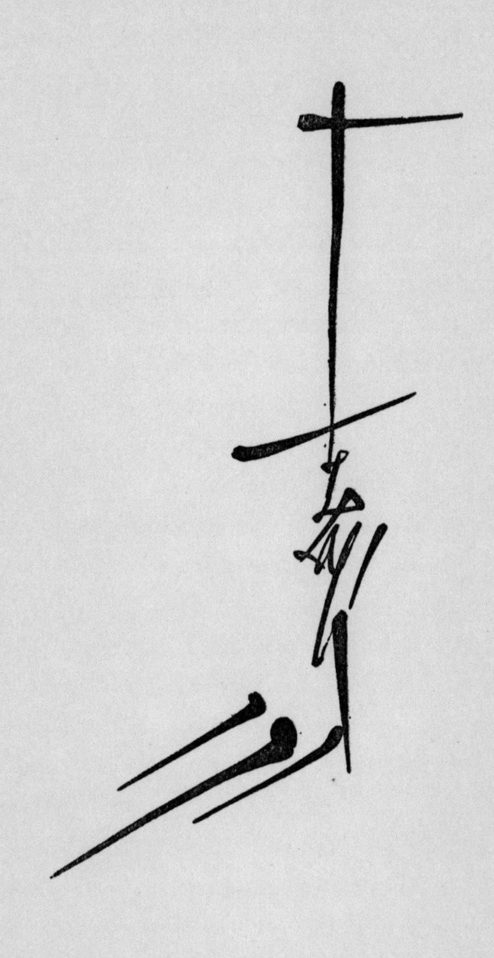

Décorativisme antidécoratif, contraire au décorativisme psychique du Modern'Style.

Apparition de l'Impérialisme Cannibale du Modern'Style

Les causes «manifestes» de production du Modern'Style nous apparaissent encore trop confuses, trop contradictoires et trop vastes pour qu'il soit question d'en trancher dans l'actualité. On pourrait en dire autant de ses causes «latentes» bien que le lecteur intelligent puisse être amené à déduire de ce qui va être dit que le mouvement qui nous occupe a eu surtout pour but d'éveiller une sorte de grande «faim originale.»

De même que la détermination de ses causes «phénoménologiques,» toute entreprise de mise au point historique en ce qui le concerne se heurterait aux plus grandes difficultés, et ceci surtout en raison de ce contradictoire et rare sentiment collectif d'individualisme féroce qui caractérise sa genèse: Bornons-nous donc à constater uniquement, aujourd'hui, le «fait» de l'apparition brusque, de l'irruption violente du Modern'Style, témoignant d'une révolution sans précédent du «sentiment d'originalité.» Le Modern'Style se présente en effet comme un bond, avec tout ce que celui-ci peut entraîner de plus cruels traumatismes pour l'art.

C'est dans l'architecture que nous allons pouvoir admirer l'ébranlement profond, dans son essence la plus consubstantiellement fonctionnaliste, de tout «élément,» fût-il le plus congénital, le plus héréditaire du passé. Avec le Modern'Style les éléments architecturaux du passé, outre qu'ils vont être soumis à la fréquente, à la totale trituration convulsive-formelle qui va

donner naissance à une nouvelle stylisation, seront appelés à revivre, à subsister couramment sous leur véritable aspect originaire, de sorte qu'en se combinant les uns avec les autres, en se fondant les uns dans les autres (en dépit de leurs antagonismes intellectuellement les plus irréconciliables, les plus irréductibles) ils vont atteindre au plus haut degré de dépréciation esthétique, manifester dans leurs rapports cette affreuse impureté qui n'a d'équivalente et d'égale que la pureté immaculée des entrelacements oniriques.

Dans un bâtiment modern'style, le gothique se métamorphose en hellénique, en extrême-oriental et, pour peu que cela passe par la tête—par une certaine fantaisie involontaire—en Renaissance qui peut à son tour devenir modern'style pur, dynamique-asymétrique (!) tout cela dans le temps et dans l'espace «débile» d'une seule fenêtre, c'est-à-dire dans ce temps et cet espace peu connus et vraisemblablement vertigineux qui, comme nous venons de l'insinuer, ne seraient autres que ceux du rêve. Tout ce qui a été le plus naturellement utilitaire et fonctionnaliste dans les architectures connues du passé, dans le Modern'Style, ne sert subitement plus à rien du tout, ou, ce qui ne saurait lui concilier l'intellectualisme pragmatiste, ne sert plus qu'au «fonctionnement des désirs,» d'ailleurs les plus troubles, disqualifiés et inavouables. De grandioses colonnes et des colonnes moyennes, inclinées, incapables de se soutenir par elles-mêmes, telles le cou fatigué des lourdes têtes hydrocéphales, émergent pour la première fois dans le monde des ondulations dures de l'eau sculptée avec le souci photographique de l'instantanéité, jusqu'alors inconnu. Elles montent par vagues des reliefs polychromes, dont l'ornementation immatérielle fige les transitions convulsives des faibles matérialisations des méta-

morphoses les plus fugitives de la fumée, ainsi que les végétaux aquatiques et la chevelure de ces femmes nouvelles, plus «appétissantes» encore que la petite soif causée par la température imaginative de la vie des extases florales où elles s'anéantissent. Ces colonnes de chair fiévreuse (37,5 degrés) ne sont destinées à soutenir rien d'autre que la fameuse libellule à l'abdomen mou et lourd comme le bloc de plomb massif où elle a été sculptée de façon subtile et éthérée, bloc de plomb de nature (par son ridicule excès de pesanteur qui introduit pourtant l'idée nécessaire de gravité) à accentuer, aggraver et compliquer avec perversité le sentiment sublime d'infinie et glaciale stérilité, à rendre plus compréhensible et plus lamentable le dynamisme irrationnel de la colonne, laquelle, par suite de toutes ces circonstances de fine ambivalence, ne peut manquer de nous apparaître comme la véritable «colonne masochiste» destinée uniquement à «se laisser dévorer par le désir,» comme la véritable première colonne molle construite et découpée dans cette réelle viande désirée vers laquelle Napoléon, comme nous savons, se dirige toujours à la tête de tous les réels et véritables impérialismes, qui, comme nous avons coutume de le répéter, ne sont autre chose que les immenses «cannibalismes de l'histoire» souvent figurés par cette côtelette concrète, grillée et savoureuse que le merveilleux matérialisme dialectique a placée, comme l'aurait fait Guillaume Tell, sur la tête même de la politique.

C'est donc à mon sens, précisément (je n'insisterai jamais assez sur ce point de vue), l'architecture tout idéale du Modern' Style qui incarnerait la plus tangible et délirante aspiration d'hyper-matérialisme. On trouvera une illustration de ce paradoxe apparent dans une comparaison courante, employée il est vrai en mauvaise part, mais pourtant si lucide, qui consiste à

assimiler une maison modern'style à un gâteau, à une tarte exhibitionniste et ornementale de «confiseur.» Je répète qu'il s'agit ici d'une comparaison lucide et intelligente, non seulement parce qu'elle dénonce le violent prosaïsme-matérialiste des besoins immédiats, urgents, sur quoi reposent les désirs idéaux, mais encore parce que, par cela même et en réalité, il est fait ainsi allusion sans euphémisme au caractère nutritif comestible de cette espèce de maisons, lesquelles ne sont autre chose que les premières maisons comestibles, que les premiers et seuls bâtiments érotisables, dont l'existence vérifie cette «fonction» urgente et si nécessaire pour l'imagination amoureuse: pouvoir le plus réellement manger l'objet du désir.

Le Modern'Style, Architecture Phénoménale. Caractéristiques générales du Phénomène

Dépréciation profonde des systèmes intellectuels.—Dépression très accentuée de l'activité raisonnante, allant jusqu'aux confins de la débilité mentale.—Imbécillité lyrique positive.—Inconscience esthétique totale.—Aucune coaction lyrique-religieuse; en revanche: échappement, liberté, développement des mécanismes inconscients.—Automatisme ornemental.—Stéréotypie.—Néologismes.—Grande névrose d'enfance, refuge dans un monde idéal, haine de la réalité, etc.—Folie des grandeurs, mégalomanie perverse, «mégalomanie objective.»—Besoin et sentiment du merveilleux et d l'originalité hyperesthétique.—Impudeur absolue de l'orgueil exhibitionnisme frénétique du «caprice» et de la «fantaisie» impérialiste.—Aucune notion de mesure.—Réalisation de désirs solidifiés.—Éclosion majestueuse aux tendances érotiques, irrationnelles, inconscientes.

Parallèle Psycho-Pathologique

Invention de la «sculpture hystérique.»—Extase érotique continue.—Contractions et attitudes sans antécédents dans l'histoire de la statuaire (il s'agit des femmes découvertes et connues après Charcot et l'école de la Salpêtrière).—Confusion et exacerbation ornementale en rapport avec les communications pathologiques; démence précoce.—Rapports étroits avec le rêve; rêveries, fantaisies diurnes.—Présence des éléments oniriques caractéristiques: condensation; déplacement, etc.—Éclosion du complexe sadique anal.—Coprophagie ornementale flagrante.—Onanisme très lent, épuisant, accompagné d'un énorme sentiment de culpabilité.

Aspirations concrètes Extra-Plastiques

Sculpture de tout l'extra-sculptural: l'eau, la fumée, les irisations de la prétuberculose et de la pollution nocturne, la femme-fleur-peau-peyotl-bijoux—nuage-flamme-papillon-miroir. Gaudi a bâti une maison selon les formes de la mer, «représentant les vagues un jour de tempête.» Une autre est faite des eaux tranquilles d'un lac. Il ne s'agit pas de décevantes métaphores, de contes de fées, etc., ces maisons existent (Paseo de Gracia à Barcelone). Il s'agit de bâtiments réels, véritable sculpture des reflets des nuages crépusculaires dans l'eau, rendue possible par le recours à une immense et insensée mosaïque multicolore et rutilante, des irisations pointillistes de laquelle émergent des formes d'eau répandue, formes d'eau se répandant, formes d'eau stagnante, formes d'eau miroitante, formes d'eau frisée par le vent, toutes ces formes d'eau construites en une succession

asymétrique et dynamique-instantanée de reliefs brisés, syncopés, enlacés, fondus par les nénuphars et nymphéas «naturalistes-stylisés» se concrétisant dans d'excentriques convergences impures et annihilatrices par d'épaisses protubérances de peur, jaillissant de la façade incroyable, contorsionnés à la fois par toute la souffrance démentielle et par tout le calme latent et infiniment doux qui n'a d'égal que celui des horrifiants floroncules apothéosiques et mûrs prêts à être mangés à la cuiller,— à la saignante, grasse et molle cuiller de viande faisandée qui approche.

Il s'est donc agi de construire un bâtiment habitable (et de plus, selon moi, comestible) avec les reflets des nuages crépusculaires sur les eaux d'un lac, l'œuvre devant en outre comporter le maximum de rigueur naturaliste et de trompe-l'œil. Je crie que c'est là un progrès gigantesque sur la simple submersion rimbaldienne du Salon au fond d'un lac.

Retour à la beauté

Le désir érotique est la ruine des esthétiques intellectualistes. Là où la Vénus de la logique s'éteint, la Vénus du «mauvais goût,» la «Vénus aux fourrures» s'annonce sous le signe de l'unique beauté, celle des réelles agitations vitales et matérialistes.—La beauté n'est que la somme de conscience de nos perversions.—Breton a dit: «La beauté sera convulsive ou ne sera pas.» Le nouvel âge surréaliste du «cannibalisme des objets» justifie également cette conclusion. «La beauté sera comestible ou ne sera pas.»

Salvador DALI.

AUJOURD'HUI, VINGT ANS APRÈS cet article du *Minotaure,* j'ai gagné la bataille Gaudi, car mes amis Alfred Barr,[1] directeur du Musée d'Art moderne de New York, et Sweeney, du Musée d'Art non objectif, ont reconnu son génie en écrivant sur lui un livre des plus importants. Et l'admiration que Le Corbusier lui-même a pour Gaudi,[2] il l'a trans-

[1] *Alfred Barr fut un ami de la première heure pour Dali. C'est lui qui le décida à venir aux États-Unis.* Dans La Vie secrète, *Dali dit de lui: «Ses gestes saccadés ressemblaient à ceux des oiseaux qui picorent. En fait, il picorait des valeurs contemporaines et sélectionnait judicieusement le bon grain de l'ivraie.»* (N. d. E.)

[2] *En 1935, lors du soulèvement de Barcelone, le corps de Gaudi fut déterré, et traîné dans les rues par des gamins. L'ami, qui décrivit la scène à Dali, ajouta que Gaudi avait l'air très bien embaumé et conservé, mais souffrait d'une mauvaise mine.* (N. d. E.)

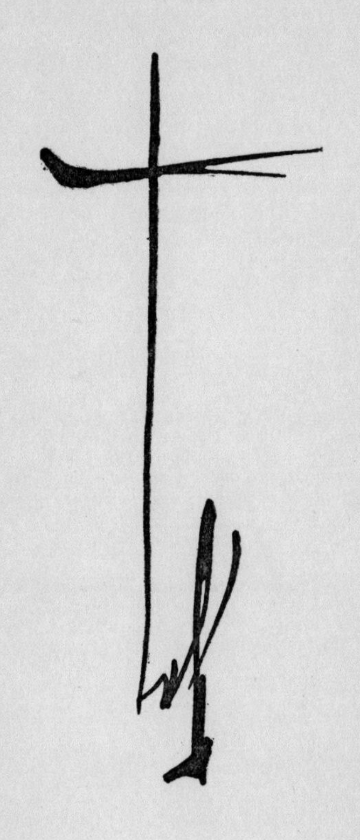

cendée dans sa propre architecture, ce qui est tout à son honneur.

Mais il est plus facile d'approcher le génie de Gaudi que celui de Raphaël, le premier étant un génie environné du tonnerre des cataclysmes et l'autre un génie baignant dans le silence céleste. Ce qu'il faut gagner désormais, c'est la bataille Raphaël, la plus décisive et la plus dure de toutes. Ce n'est que dans la juste appréciation de Raphaël que l'on reconnaîtra les vrais esprits supérieurs de notre époque, puisque Raphaël est le plus antiacadémique, le plus tendrement vivant et le plus futuriste de tous les archétypes esthétiques de tous les temps.

Je demande à mes amis Le Corbusier, Barr et Sweeney, et surtout à Malraux, qu'ils s'arrêtent un instant pour examiner combien a vieilli physiquement et moralement un de ces papiers collés, jaune, anecdotique, littéraire et sentimental de l'époque cubiste! Qu'ils le comparent au petit saint Georges de Raphaël[3] resté frais comme une rose! Mais je doute du résultat, car ces quatre-là sont encore trop du côté du cataclysme!

Cataclysme ou ciel, peu importe, nos modernes ne pouvaient supporter les moindres vestiges d'ornementation dans leurs «machines à habiter» et ils se sont trouvés envahis par l'académisme abstrait qui n'est que du très médiocre art pseudo-décoratif.

Nos modernes dont les cheveux se hérissent d'horreur à l'idée d'une matière qui ne serait pas aseptique et préfabriquée n'ont pas eu à attendre la fin de leur vie pour voir l'apothéose du folklore le plus naïf, la résurrection de tous les plagiats, de tous les archéologismes de tous les temps, à la seule condition qu'ils soient éclaboussés et mal foutus. Chaque tableau, chaque

[3] *De la collection Mellon à Washington.* (N. d. E.)

céramique, chaque tapis moderne qui se respecte doit sembler sortir d'une excavation et simuler les accidents de la patine et de la décrépitude truculente. Et cela, à un point que l'on ne se serait même pas permis au temps des déjà regrettés «buffets Michel-Ange,» où l'on se contentait d'imiter de modestes vermoulures.

Enfin, qu'y a-t-il de plus cocu, de plus trompé, de plus accablé de fissures et de craquelures que cet art moderne fanatique de la propreté stérilisée des formes fonctionnelles et des surfaces aseptiques, alors qu'on le croirait assiégé par la peste et trouvé par l'ironie du destin, comme on dit, dans ces poubelles où l'Italien Burri ramasse des linges sanguinolents. Bien qu'éternellement et allégrement cocu, Burri n'en suspend pas moins au-dessus de sa tête ces ordures qui ont la forme du plus dépressif de tous les «mobiles» pareils à ceux que fabrique spécialement pour lui un «premier prix» de sculpture moderne—moderne.

Partisans de l'ultra-neuf, snobés par les parvenus du pseudo vieux-vieux, les critiques dithyrambiques ont été abusés par la technique; avec l'Impressionnisme la décadence de l'art pictural est devenue . . . impressionnante.

Paul Cézanne—un des peintres les plus merveilleusement réactionnaires de tous les temps—était aussi l'un des plus «impérialistes,» puisqu'il voulait refaire Poussin «d'après nature,» donc d'après la nouvelle conception de la discontinuité de la matière, grande vérité du divisionnisme dionysiaque de l'Impressionnisme. Il est malheureux que son élan apollinien[4] ait été desservi par sa maladresse fatale. Sa gaucherie n'a pour

[4] *Est-il besoin de rappeler que, dans la philosophie de Nietzsche, est «apollinien» qui possède la faculté de créer les images réelles. Alors que, dans la même philosophie, «dionysiaque» se dit de l'état où l'homme a conscience de soi comme capable de représentation ou d'intelligence.* (N. d. E.)

pendant que la virtuosité délirante de Velasquez. Il aurait fallu que ce fût Velasquez qui, comme Bonaparte, coule l'anarchie de la peinture orgiaque dans l'empire césarien des formes, en y ajoutant cette notion de la nature discontinue qui manquait à Poussin.

Mais, pour pathétique que cela soit, jamais Cézanne ne réussit à peindre une seule pomme ronde capable de recéler—monarchiquement—dans son volume absolu les cinq corps réguliers.[5]

Les critiques dithyrambiques, en complet accord avec la médiocrité des peintres cézanniens, ne surent que poser en impératifs catégoriques les déficiences, les gaucheries et les maladresses catastrophiques du maître. Devant cette débâcle totale des moyens d'expression, on crut avoir fait un pas en avant vers la libération de la technique picturale. Chaque échec fut baptisé économie, intensité, plasticité,—et quand on prononce cet horrible mot de «plasticité,» c'est que les vers sont là!

Enfin, trompés mais gais à leur habitude, les critiques dithyrambiques, au lieu de se trouver en possession de la nobilissime corbeille de pommes intactes et divines—symbole d'un nouvel âge d'or cézannien—, restèrent tout simplement seuls avec une corbeille remplie de leur propre merde.[6] Et comme, même pour tresser avec dignité une simple corbeille, une certaine technique reste indispensable, ils n'avaient réussi qu'à se confectionner une espèce de panier tout à fait indigne de ce nom.

[5] *C'est-à-dire: le cube, le tétraèdre, le dodécaèdre, l'hexaèdre et l'octaèdre.* (N. d. E.)

[6] *«A Rome on ne se faisait point difficulté de parler de merde. Horace, le délicat Horace, et tous les poètes du siècle d'Auguste en parlent en cent endroits de leurs ouvrages»* (comte de Caylus).

Jamais l'expression de Michel de Montaigne «chier[7] dans le panier et puis se le mettre sur la tête,» ne pourra être plus sagement appliquée qu'à ces critiques dithyrambiques de la nouvelle technique des peintres modernes.

A peine avaient-ils été trompés successivement par la «laideur» et le «moderne,» puis par la «technique,» que nos critiques dithyrambiques furent de nouveau, sans qu'on leur laissât de répit, cocufiés sur l'heure par l' «art abstrait.» Mais cette fois le cocufiage fut colossal, totalitaire, impérial, je dirais presque cosmique, et ceci autant du côté spirituel (à ce point anéanti que rien de pire ne pouvait lui arriver) que du côté temporel, car ce n'est plus un mystère que ceux qui avaient mis là leur confiance sont en train d'y perdre tout leur argent, signe certain de banqueroute.

La tromperie commença avec Picasso dont le sang andalou charriait des morceaux de ce monument d'iconoclastie qu'est l'Alhambra de Grenade. Puis le cubisme s'employa à fragmenter la matière, en utilisant encore les matériaux du «maçon néo-platonicien» dont Cézanne se servait pour faire tenir debout ses maisons. A cela, le cubisme devait ajouter un peu de ciment de Huerta del Ebro en Aragon, car la terre d'Aragon est la plus férocement réaliste et concrète du monde.

Il n'est pas difficile, en récapitulant, de voir que les matériaux utilisés par Cézanne, plus ces matériaux fournis au cubisme par la terre d'Aragon, étaient catholiques par excellence, et que c'est seulement avec eux qu'on allait pouvoir se permettre de

[7] *Autre exemple de l'emploi de ce mot rare: «Ci-gît un roi, par grand merveille, qui mourut, comme Dieu permet, d'un coup de serpe et d'une vieille, comme il chiait dans une met»* (d'Aubigné).

peindre la réalité. Une certaine coquetterie arabe se révélerait, de plus, parfaitement adéquate pour fragmenter la forme hispano-mauresque trop sèche et trop pelée, de même que les impressionnistes avaient décomposé la lumière avec la subtilité humide qui tombe des ciels de Delft. Comment aussi ne pas retrouver cette subtilité dans les réminiscences et les regrets maternels et atlantiques de Velasquez, dont la mère était portugaise, ce qui explique le miracle de la peinture du plus grand de tous les artistes: le sexe de la Castille toujours mouillé par une éjaculation que seules les veines granitiques de l'Espagne pouvaient conduire par de mystérieux réseaux jusqu'à la pupille du peintre.

Le cubisme n'était et ne restera donc que comme le plus héroïque effort pour garder la figure (génie et figure jusqu'à la sépulture) au moment où l'on acquérait une pleine conscience de la nouvelle discontinuité de la matière. En fait, il continuait de s'agir d'objets, toujours d'objets, d'objets concrets et anecdotiques qui en arrivaient à porter sur eux, bien collées, les étiquettes de leur propre anecdote sentimentale. Les guitares sont en ciment, leurs arêtes coupent les mains et les visages avec le grincement objectif de leurs structures. Tant d'objectivité portée à son paroxysme ne crève pas les yeux des esthéticiens qui, au lieu d'une révolte objective, croient à une étape vers l'abstrait.

Il n'y a là rien que de normal et Picasso, un jour, m'a avoué dans l'intimité qu'aucun des panégyristes de son cubisme gris n'avait jamais été foutu de voir ce que ses tableaux représentaient. Ainsi de ces monstrueux académismes sont nés tous les néo-plasticismes et notamment cet exemple dégradant de

débilité mentale qu'on appelait pompeusement «*abstraction-création.*»

Et l'on entendra le Piet, Piet, Piet des nouveaux académiciens modernes. Ce Piet Mondrian avait, pourtant, une faiblesse pour Dali. Il disait que personne au monde n'était capable comme moi de placer une petite pierre qui projette son ombre dans l'espace d'un tableau. Moi, j'ai une faiblesse pour Mondrian, car, adorant Vermeer, je trouve dans l'ordre de Mondrian la propreté de femme de chambre de Vermeer, et même sa rétinienne instantanéité des bleus et des jaunes. Je ne m'empresse pas moins de dire que Vermeer est presque tout et Mondrian presque rien!

Des critiques complètement crétins ont employé pendant plusieurs années le nom de Piet Mondrian comme s'il représentait le summum de toute activité spirituelle. Ils le citaient à tout propos. Piet pour l'architecture, Piet pour la poésie, Piet pour le mysticisme, Piet pour la philosophie, les blancs de Piet, les jaunes de Piet, Piet, Piet, Piet,. . . . .
Piet, Piet, Piet, Piépie, Pitié, Piet. Eh bien! Piet, c'est moi Salvador qui vous le dis, avec un «i» de moins, ce n'eût été qu'un pet.[8]

[8] «*Soudain Epistémon commence à respirer, puis ouvrir les yeux, puis bâiller, puis éternuer, puis fit un gros pet de ménage.*» (Rabelais, II, 30).

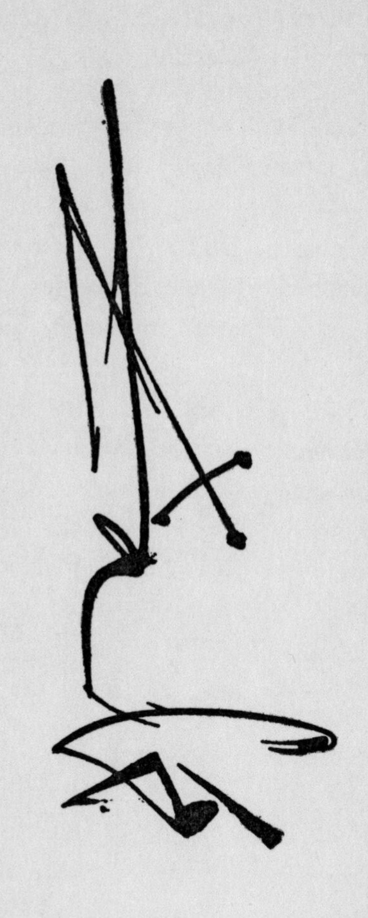

UNE JOTA ARAGONAISE A POUR refrain strident, ce cri viscéral, ibérique et irrationnel:

> Je t'aime comme on aime sa mère
> comme on aime l'argent!

Ce qui me plaît le plus de toute la pensée d'Auguste Comte, c'est le moment précis où, avant de fonder sa nouvelle religion positiviste, il place, au sommet de sa hiérarchie, les banquiers auxquels il accorde une importance capitale. Peut-être est-ce là le côté phénicien de mon sang ampurdan, mais j'ai toujours été ébloui par l'or sous quelque forme qu'il se présente. Ayant, dès mon adolescence, appris que Miguel de Cervantes, après avoir écrit pour la plus grande gloire de l'Espagne son immortel *Don Quichotte,* mourut dans la misère noire, que Christophe Colomb, après avoir découvert le Nouveau Monde, était mort aussi dans

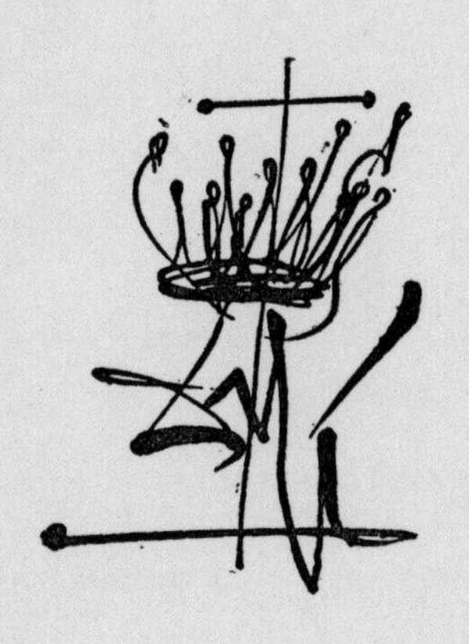

les mêmes conditions et de plus en prison, dès mon adolescence, dis-je, ma prudence me conseilla fortement deux choses:

1) de faire ma prison le plus tôt possible. Et ce fut fait.

2) de devenir autant que possible légèrement multimillionnaire. Et cela aussi est fait.

La façon la plus simple de refuser toute concession à l'or, c'est d'en avoir soi-même. Avec de l'or, il devient tout à fait inutile de «s'engager.» Un héros ne s'engage nulle part! Il est tout le contraire du domestique. Il faut vraiment avoir les dents couvertes de Sartre pour ne pas oser parler ainsi! Donc soyons prudent, comme le recommande Saint-Granier, si nous voulons nous permettre d'être nietzschéens. Toutes les valeurs concrètes de la peinture moderne resteront éternellement traduisibles sur le plan matériel en cette chose que moi personnellement, j'ai toujours aimée: l'*argent*![1]

En revanche, que se rassurent les critiques purs qui ont sans cesse méprisé l'argent et ont eu peur de se salir en le touchant: les valeurs abstraites qu'ils défendent dans la peinture moderne se convertiront inéluctablement en argent tout à fait propre, totalement inoffensif et immatériel. Ce sera de l'argent purement abstrait.

[1] *On sait qu'André Breton avait baptisé Salvador Dali «Avida Dollars.» Dali assure que cette anagramme fut son talisman qui rendit «fluide, douce et monotone la pluie des dollars.» Il s'est promis de raconter un jour toute la vérité sur ce dérèglement béni de Danaé. Ce sera un chapitre d'un nouveau livre intitulé «De la vie de Salvador Dali considérée comme un chef-d'œuvre»* (N. d. E.)

FIN

S.S. AMERICA

EN ROUTE VERS LE HAVRE. AVRIL 1956.

ÉPILOGUE

De toute la révolution moderne une seule idée n'a pas vieilli et reste si vivante qu'elle sera le fondement du nouveau classicisme que l'on attend de façon imminente. Aucun des critiques dithyrambiques du vieil art moderne ne l'a encore remarqué. Il s'agit de rien moins que le fameux *d'après nature* de Paul Cézanne.[1]

La discontinuité de la matière

La découverte la plus transcendante de notre époque est celle de la physique nucléaire sur la constitution de la matière. La matière est discontinue et toute expérience valable dans la peinture moderne ne peut et ne doit partir que d'une seule idée aussi concrète que significative: *la discontinuité de la matière.*

Cette discontinuité est annoncée pour la première fois dans l'histoire de l'art par les touches corpusculaires de Vermeer et les coups de pinceau en l'air de Velasquez. De même, c'est

[1] *La nature est le nom que le peintre donne à la physique.* (N. d. E.)

l'impressionnisme qui a inventé pour la première fois la division de la lumière. Les confetti chromosomatiques de Seurat sont l'acte notarié de la discontinuité de la matière. La collision sadique des complémentaires dans le périmètre—bosselé par le mouvement brownien—des pommes de Cézanne, ne sont que les manifestations physiques du mouvement de la matière discontinue.

Dans le cubisme gris de Picasso, le morcellement réintégratif de la réalité n'est qu'un exemple de la volonté féroce de cette réalité pour garder un aspect figuratif en pleine discontinuité de la matière. Les déchirements viscéraux du génial Boccioni sont l'annonce anticipée du dynamisme supersonique et les apollons glorieux de la discontinuité de la matière. Le «Roi et la Reine» de Duchamp peuvent être traversés par nous en vitesse à cause de la discontinuité de la matière. Les montres de Dali sont molles parce qu'elles sont le produit masochiste de la discontinuité de la matière. Les signes de Mathieu sont les décrets royaux de la discontinuité de la matière.

Le grouillement dionysiaque est là, mais toute cette hétérogénéité héroïque ne vaudra esthétiquement rien tant que n'aura pas été trouvée la forme artistique et classique d'une cosmogonie apollinienne.

Pour que les forces vitalement hétérogènes et antiacadémiques de l'art moderne ne périssent pas dans le ridicule anecdotique du simple dilettantisme expérimental et narcissique, il faut trois choses essentielles:

1° Du talent et de préférence du génie.[2]

[2] *Depuis la Révolution française, se développe une vicieuse tendance crétinisante qui consiste à considérer que les génies (à part leur œuvre) sont en tout des êtres plus ou moins semblables au reste du commun des mortels. Cette cro-*

2° Réapprendre à peindre aussi bien que Velasquez et de préférence comme Vermeer.[3]

3° Posséder une cosmogonie monarchique et catholique aussi absolue que possible et à tendances impérialistes.

C'est seulement alors que, nietzschéens à l'envers, c'est-à-dire aspirant vers le sublime, nous observerons à l'œil nu «d'après nature,» *l'archange antiprotonique* si divinement éclaté que nous pourrons enfin plonger nos mains de peintre entre les chromosomes *fissionnés* de sa substance rossignolesque pour toucher de nos doigts douloureux et gonflés de sang le trésor discontinu et désiré depuis notre propre jeunesse. Et, croyant comme Soeringe que nous commandons tout par notre volonté de puissance en puissance, je sais que nous toucherons alors notre propre divinité de peintres.[4]

Lu, approuvé et signé:
Salvador DALI.

---

yance est fausse. Je l'affirme pour moi qui suis le génie moderne par excellence. (S. D.)

[3] *Dans son* Manifeste mystique *paru en 1952, Dali disait déjà aux peintres: «Peintres, peignez méticuleusement, avec autant de réalité qu'une photo en couleurs, que votre main se conduise comme un stroboscope, et alors je vous promets qu'à partir de ce moment vos tableaux risqueront de devenir immortels!»* (N. d. E.)

[4] *Comme on a peut-être pu s'en rendre compte, Dali écrivain ne ménage pas son admiration à Dali peintre, mais c'est parce qu'il est persuadé de la supériorité «monarchique» du peintre, en général. Il y a trois ans, la Fédération anarchiste ibérique publiait un manifeste pour annoncer son ralliement à la monarchie espagnole, car, spécifiait-on, les peintres sont des monarques. Dali a retrouvé là une de ses idées les plus chères: il n'y a de réelle liberté que sous l'autorité d'un monarque. Dans son enfance, il a beaucoup aimé porter un déguisement de roi, mais ce n'est pas à ce titre qu'il aspire pour lui-même, c'est à celui que lui confère son prénom: Salvador, le sauveur de la peinture. Dans son* Journal d'un génie, *encore inédit, il note, entre autres choses: «Avant de m'endormir, au lieu de me frotter les mains (ce geste abominable serait typiquement antidalinien) je me les embrasse avec une joie très pure, tout en me disant que l'univers est peu de chose en comparaison de l'ampleur d'un front peint par Raphaël.»* (N. d. E.)

APPENDICE I

La lucidité de Dali quand il parle peinture a de quoi décourager les critiques qui n'abordent jamais la question que de l'extérieur. A une enquête sur l'émancipation de la peinture, Dali répondait déjà en 1934:

«Si je dois m'exprimer brièvement sur les questions du «modèle,» de la «spontanéité» et du «hasard» dans l'œuvre peinte, je dirai que selon moi—et pour tenter de rendre ce peu de mots le plus substantiel possible—le «modèle» ne serait pour le peintre qu'un succulent et gélatineux «pied de porc gratiné» dans lequel, comme chacun sait, la viande molle et superfine ne fait qu'envelopper de ses «délires de douceur nutritive» le véritable et authentique os pelé de l'objectivité. Mais le mieux gratiné et le plus savoureux de tous les pieds de porc, qui, pour peu qu'on fasse appel à la mémoire, est celui du «réalisme,» se trouve avoir été flairé depuis des siècles par les nez fins des peintres hollandais et mangé en fin de compte par Vermeer de Delft, lequel ne laissa que l'os refroidi, pour permettre au grand

Meissonnier de trouver en le léchant les dernières douceurs fines. S'il n'y a plus de nos jours de «modèle,» il y a tout lieu de penser que c'est le peintre qui l'a mangé, et ceci est trop généralement et trop populairement admis pour que j'insiste sur l'inévitable nostalgie de tout peintre devant tout modèle. Comment le pied de porc en question existerait-il encore aujourd'hui, quand on sait que les surréalistes, dépassant le cannibalisme de la viande sont passés à celui des os, pour en venir à dévorer les objets et les êtres-objets? C'est assez dire que le modèle ne saurait exister pour moi qu'en tant que métaphore intestinale. Non seulement le modèle, mais encore l'objectivité même a été mangée. Je ne puis donc peindre que d'après certains systèmes de délire de la digestion.

«En ce qui concerne la spontanéité, je dirai qu'elle est aussi un pied de porc, mais un pied de porc à l'envers, c'est-à-dire une langouste, celle-ci, comme chacun sait, présentant, au contraire du pied de porc, un squelette extérieur, alors que la viande superfine et délicate, c'est-à-dire le délire, occupe l'intérieur, ce qui signifie—pour parler d'un seul jet et sans euphémisme—que, pour la spontanéité, la carapace de l'objectivité offre une résistance au délire mou de la viande; que, pour parvenir à celle-ci, on perd souvent du temps et qu'on n'y parvient d'ailleurs que pour constater que la viande qu'on découvre n'a plus d'os. Toutes ces considérations m'entraînent à me méfier, en général, de la «spontanéité» à l'état pur, dans laquelle je retrouve toujours le goût conventionnel et stéréotypé de l'invariable langouste de restaurant et à préférer personnellement à la spontanéité la «systématisation» qui, à l'exemple du délire paranoïaque, peut se produire et de fait se produit «spontanément»—la «spontanéité» en question ayant cessé de prétendre à l'*objectivité introuvable,* d'autant plus que celle-ci a été préalablement détruite comme on a vu pour la langouste, mais impliquant au contraire cette douceur supplémentaire, la plus fine de toutes, qui réside dans le goût et même dans le contact de la viande qu'on peut encore trouver et qu'on trouve à l'intérieur des os quand, l'os rongé, arrive le moment de s'attaquer à celui-ci. C'est précisément au moment algide où l'on atteint la moelle même de l'imagination qu'on a le droit de supposer qu'on domine (et qu'effectivement on domine) la situation.

«Si le «modèle» est un pied de porc gratiné et la spontanéité une langouste, le hasard pourrait bien n'être qu'une sérieuse et importante côtelette grillée, pétillante de saveur et d'arrière-pensées biologiques, je le dis parce que le hasard figure et constitue exactement ce point moyen de douceur entre le «modèle» et la «spontanéité,» c'est-à-dire entre le pied de porc gratiné et la langouste à l'américaine. On observera, en effet, que si dans le pied de porc les os sont à l'intérieur de la viande et dans la langouste la viande à l'intérieur du squelette, dans le cas de la côtelette les os sont moitié à l'intérieur, moitié à l'extérieur, c'est-à-dire coexistent, et que l'os et la viande, objectivité et délire, se montrant visiblement en même temps, ne font autre chose qu'énoncer cette vérité que je ne me lasserai jamais de répéter, à savoir que le hasard n'est autre chose que le résultat d'une activité irrationnelle systématique (paranoïaque) ; ce qui, pour revenir à nos obsessions comestibles et à notre vocabulaire emprunté à la nutrition, peut se résumer dans l'idée que le hasard, tel qu'il intervient dans le phénomène artistique n'est que l'expression du conflit terriblement excitant pour la famine, qui résulte de notre mise en présence simultanée de l'os et de la viande, précisons une fois de plus: de l'objectivité et du délire, envenimé encore de cette ardeur de la grillade qui brûle les dents (toute côtelette grillée digne de ce nom devant être mangée à brûledents, mais ceci est une autre question) et quand je dis: qui brûle les dents, je veux dire: qui brûle l'imagination.»

APPENDICE II

Autour d'un Film a Naître

En 1954 au Musée du Louvre, Salvador Dali exécute une copie de *La Dentellière* de Vermeer de Delft, tableau dont la puissance agressive l'obsède depuis son enfance. Sur la toile, Dali peint des cornes de rhinocéros qu'il continuera au printemps suivant, mais cette fois au Zoo de Vincennes devant un rhinocéros vivant. De retour en Espagne, il termine pendant l'été 1955 cette copie rhinocérontique et corpusculaire pour, en décembre de la même année, faire une communication à Paris en Sorbonne, destinée à expliquer les affinités morphologiques d'une part et cosmogoniques[1] d'autre part, découvertes par lui entre *La Dentellière,* le rhinocéros, le tournesol et le chou-fleur.

Dès la visite au Musée du Louvre, Robert Descharnes avait entrepris la réalisation d'un film: «Histoire prodigieuse de *La*

[1] *Par cosmogoniques, il faut entendre: de la cosmogonie (ou mythologie) propre à Dali.* (N. d. E.)

Dentellière et du rhinocéros,» en filmant et enregistrant depuis cette date toutes les recherches et actions délirantes et systématiques de Salvador Dali.

Dans cette «aventure» cinématographique, si l'évolution de Salvador Dali peintre est décrite à l'aide d'un certain nombre de plans de ses toiles les plus importantes de l'époque surréaliste à aujourd'hui, il ne s'agit pourtant pas d'un film sur sa peinture elle-même, mais plutôt sur l'évolution de Dali, du surréalisme à sa peinture actuelle (et de ce fait à son attitude en face de la peinture contemporaine).

Grâce à la collaboration de Dali, à son génie des correspondances et à cette extraordinaire systématisation de son délire, «l'Histoire prodigieuse de *La Dentellière* et du rhinocéros» sera le premier film réalisé sur l'activité paranoïaque critique;[2] Robert Descharnes tente d'en montrer le déroulement dans la vie de Dali et d'expliquer l'application de cette méthode tant à sa peinture qu'à des recherches parallèles, comme celles qui mènent de *La Dentellière* de Vermeer à la chair de poule[3] par le rhinocéros et le chou-fleur.

Afin que les prises de vues destinées à montrer ce génie des correspondances et des images doubles[4] gardent toute leur efficacité visuelle, les truquages et effets cinématographiques habituels ont été systématiquement écartés.

[2] *Méthode spontanée de connaissance irrationnelle fondée sur l'association interprétative critique des phénomènes délirants.* (N. d. E.)

[3] *Pour Dali c'est d'abord le côté divisionniste corpusculaire qui est le lien entre Vermeer et cette chair de poule* microphysique. (N. d. E.)

[4] *«C'est par un processus nettement paranoïaque qu'il est possible d'obtenir une image double, c'est-à-dire la présentation d'un objet qui, sans la moindre modification figurative ou anatomique, soit en même temps la représentation d'un autre objet absolument différent, dénuée elle aussi de tout genre de déformation ou anormalité qui pourrait déceler quelque arrangement.»* (*René Crevel:* Dali ou l'anti-obscurantisme.)

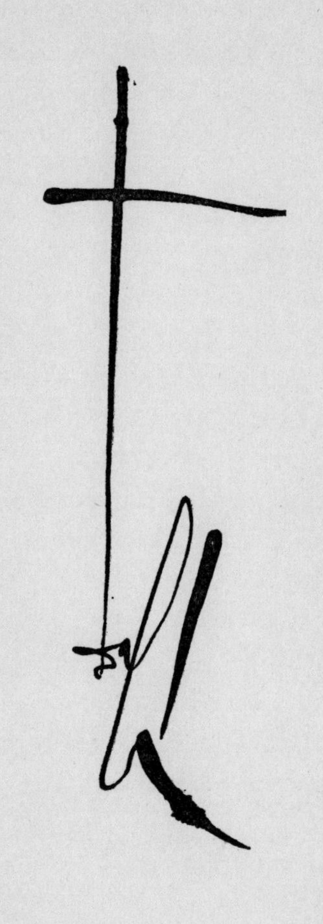